D1375794

THE HAMLYN LECTURES
FORTY-SEVENTH SERIES

TURNING POINTS OF THE COMMON LAW

AUSTRALIA
LBC Information Services—Sydney

CANADA and USA
Carswell—Toronto

NEW ZEALAND
Brooker's—Auckland

SINGAPORE and MALAYSIA
Thomson Information (S.E. Asia)—Singapore

TURNING POINTS OF THE COMMON LAW

by

THE RT HON. THE LORD COOKE OF THORNDON
KBE

Published under the auspices of
THE HAMLYN TRUST

LONDON
SWEET & MAXWELL
1997

Published in 1997 by Sweet & Maxwell Limited of
100 Avenue Road, Swiss Cottage,
London NW3 3PF
Typeset by Selwood Systems,
Midsomer Norton
Printed in England by
Clays Ltd, St Ives plc

No natural forests were destroyed to make this product;
only farmed timber was used and replanted

**A CIP catalogue record for this book is available from the British
Library**

ISBN 0 421 598 603 (HB)
0 421 598 700 (PB)

All rights reserved. UK statutory material in this publication
is acknowledged as Crown copyright.
No part of this publication may be reproduced or transmitted
in any form or by any means, or stored in any retrieval system
of any nature without prior written permission,
except for permitted fair dealing under the Copyright, Designs and
Patents Act 1988,
or in accordance with the terms of a licence issued by the
Copyright Licensing Agency in respect of a photocopying and/or
reprographic reproduction. Application for
permission for other use of copyright material
including permission to reproduce extracts in other
published works shall be made
to the publishers. Full acknowledgement of author, publisher
and source must be given.

11761431

UNIVERSITY OF GLAMORGAN
PRIFYSGOL MORGANNWG

Learning Resources
Centre

©
Robin Cooke
1997

TABLE OF CONTENTS

THE HAMLYN LECTURES

The Hamlyn Lectures

The Hamlyn Lectures

The Hamlyn Lectures

THE HAMLYN TRUST

The Hamlyn Trust owes its existence to the will of the late Miss Emma Warburton Hamlyn of Torquay, who died in 1941 at the age of 80. She came of an old and well-known Devon family. Her father, William Bussell Hamlyn, practised in Torquay as a solicitor and J.P. for many years, and it seems likely that Miss Hamlyn founded the trust in his memory. Emma Hamlyn was a woman of strong character, intelligent and cultured, well-versed in literature, music and art, and a lover of her country. She travelled extensively in Europe and Egypt, and apparently took considerable interest in the law and ethnology of the countries and cultures that she visited. An account of Miss Hamlyn by Dr Chantal Stebbings of the University of Exeter may be found, under the title "The Hamlyn Legacy," in volume 42 of the published lectures.

Miss Hamlyn bequeathed the residue of her estate on trust in terms which it seems were her own. The wording was thought to be vague, and the will was taken to the Chancery Division of the High Court, which in November 1948 approved a Scheme for the administration of the trust. Paragraph 3 of the Scheme, which closely follows Miss Hamlyn's own wording, is as follows:

> "The object of the charity is the furtherance by lectures or otherwise among the Common People of the United Kingdom of Great Britain and Northern Ireland of the knowledge of the Comparative Jurisprudence and Ethnology of the Chief European countries including the United Kingdom, and the circumstances of the growth of such jurisprudence to the Intent that the Common People of the United Kingdom may realise the privileges which in law and custom they enjoy in comparison with other European Peoples and realising and appreciating such privileges may recognise the responsibilities and obligations attaching to them."

The Trustees are to include the Vice-Chancellor of the University of Exeter, representatives of the Universities of London, Leeds,

Glasgow, Belfast and Wales and persons co-opted. At present there are nine Trustees:

Professor J.A. Andrews, M.A., B.C.L.
Professor T.C. Daintith, M.A.
Professor D.S. Greer, LL.D., B.C.L. (Chairman)
Sir Geoffrey Holland, K.C.B., M.A. (Oxon.)
Mr. P.J. Seago, J.P., LL.M.
Professor A.J. Ogus, M.A., B.C.L.
Professor J.P. Grant, LL.M.
Professor D.E.C. Wedderburn, M.A., D.Litt.
Rt. Hon. The Lord Browne-Wilkinson

From the outset it was decided that the Trust's objects could best be achieved by means of an annual course of public lectures of outstanding interest and quality by eminent Lecturers, and by their subsequent publication and distribution to a wider audience. Details of these Lectures are given on pages vii–x. In recent years, however, the Trustees have expanded their activities by setting up a "small grants" scheme to provide financial support for other activities designed to further public understanding of the law, and they will shortly be making a number of special awards under this scheme to mark the 50th Anniversary of the first series of Hamlyn Lectures delivered by the Rt. Hon. Lord Justice Denning (as he then was) in October and November 1949.

The forty-eighth series of Lectures consisted of four lectures delivered by the Rt. Hon. The Lord Cooke of Thorndon on four successive Thursdays in November 1996, in the Inner Temple, De Montfort University, the University of Cambridge and the University of Oxford respectively.

March 1997   **DESMOND GREER**
                                                      Chairman of the Trustees

PREFACE

Different kinds of writing on the law call for different techniques. Judgments must usually be fact-specific and concise; the Judge is supposed to be cautious about generalisations and self-disciplined as to obiter. Textbook-writing requires above all comprehensiveness and accuracy rather than a parade of personal opinions. On the other hand, articles allow full scope for the latter and are often most effective when they argue closely a distinctive point of view on a limited theme.

A series of public lectures to mixed audiences—some members already full of learning and wisdom, others merely aspiring to that condition—probably needs something different again. At all events I have assumed licence to be neither narrowly-focused nor comprehensive nor disciplined. The collection might have been called *A Ramble Round the Classics*, but for a hint of plagiarism of two distingushed Caius scholars, Michael Oakeshott and Guy Griffith, whose *A Guide to the Classics* turned out to be about horse-racing.

The lectures were given in the Michaelmas Term 1996 at four venues. I am most grateful to the governing bodies of the Inner Temple, the De Montfort and Cambridge Law Schools, and All Souls College, Oxford. The Hamlyn Trustees, and particularly the chairman, Professor Desmond Greer, have been fully supportive, as have the publishers, Sweet & Maxwell. The typing was begun in Wellington by my secretary, Dale Densem (who also undertook the initial proof-reading) but most of it was done in London by one of the secretaries to the Lords of Appeal, Marilyn Byatt. I have been the fortunate beneficiary of the outstanding technical and managerial skills of both of them.

The crossword, the relevance of which is explained at the beginning of the fourth lecture, is reproduced by kind permission of *The Times*. For those who prefer not to be troubled to do it, the answers appear on a separate page, with the questions conveying a message ringed. Compiling this crossword must have been an effort; I understand that the editor is about to get some energy back (5).

Last I would thank the audiences. Let Lord Lloyd of Berwick (Eton and Trinity, Cambridge) be taken as an unduly flattering representative. He wrote—

Omne tulit punctum qui miscuit utile dulci,
Lectorem delectando pariterque monendo

To which the reply had to be—

Principibus placuisse viris non ultima laus est
Non cuivis homini contingit adire Corinthum.

Whether Miss Hamlyn would have approved of Horace before her lectures is doubtful, but she might have been placated by learning that translations are to be found in the Oxford Dictionary of Quotations.

Robin Cooke
Wellington
New Zealand
December 1996

TABLE OF CASES

Table of Cases

Table of Cases

Table of Cases

Table of Cases

A Real Thing

Salomon v. A. Salomon & Co. Ltd
[1897] A.C. 22, 33, per Lord Halsbury L.C.

INTRODUCTION

Almost all English-speaking lawyers know that the first Hamlyn lectures were given by Lord Justice Denning, as he then was. They were delivered in his own Inn, Lincoln's Inn, in 1949. I have the privilege this evening of beginning this season's series with a message from him. He sends his affectionate good wishes to all his friends in the Inner Temple (of which, like the Middle Temple and Gray's Inn, he is an Honorary Bencher) and recalls being pleased at the general reception which his lectures received. I understand that this enthusiasm was not shared in all high places. Perhaps Sir Stephen Sedley will illuminate that point when he delivers the fiftieth series of the lectures in 1998. Lord Denning adds that it was these lectures that made him well known to the general public.

Turning to another great Englishman, as a schoolboy in New Zealand I was fascinated by Lord Macaulay. The style was the man. If, even then, I had any subliminal suspicion that sometimes it verged on claptrap, this was suppressed. For a youth there was a thrilling panache about his incisive antithetical narrative, its vigour reflecting the headlong pace of his drafting. As every schoolboy once knew, his chief work begins "I purpose to write the history of England from the accession of King James the Second down to a time which is within the memory of men still living ... I shall recount the errors ... I shall trace the course ... I shall relate how ..." and so forth. Miss Hamlyn would presumably have approved of his superb confidence in the superiority of British institutions (recounted errors notwith-standing).

She would have been gratified also that Macaulay was a best-seller addressing the Common People of the United Kingdom. In these lectures I shall seek to comply with her directions by not pitching the discourse only to the subclass of the clerisy who read the *Law Quarterly Review*, while gratefully acknowledging the distinguished presence of a number of them this evening. As to the subject-matter, I shall conform to the terms of the Trust up to a point: that is to say by speaking of some of the circumstances of the growth of United Kingdom jurisprudence. And I shall conform to that youthful influence by copying the first two words of Macaulay's History.

I purpose, then, to focus in turn on four great cases, each beyond doubt a decisive turning point in the evolution of the common law. Although in diverse fields of law, they are all familiar in broad outline to every lawyer. So the subject can be called trite. Nonetheless, amid the overwhelming mass of case law, mushrooming daily beyond the manageable compass of anyone, there is a value in returning from time to time to truly first principles. The eve of the twenty-first century is a good time to think about past landmarks and their continuing significance. Of the four cases, one will be a hundred years old next week, while the youngest of the others is already approaching thirty. Yet their sway is undiminished, indeed growing.

Further, I purpose to try to analyse the issues and the decisions in these great cases from a point of view differing in two ways from those of many of the legal scholars who have written about them. First, I shall speak primarily as a still working Judge interested in learning how leading judicial craftsmen have solved problems. I believe that in milestone appellate decisions there is usually one motivating idea which is found to prevail over all others. To identify this may be useful, for it may throw light on the utility or proper scope of a principle.

Secondly, I shall introduce a Commonwealth dimension. The terms of the Hamlyn Trust ignore the Commonwealth and the United States. The Trust is Euro-centred. An unremitting approach of that kind would no longer be feasible, if only because Commonwealth case law is beginning to have some impact in the shaping of English common law; to the extent at least that an English judge, if a Commonwealth decision has come to attention, will buttress a judgment with it if it proceeds on an attractive line of approach. And sometimes a general trend in Commonwealth jurisdictions carries weight.[1]

It is true that a number of earlier Hamlyn lecturers have spoken about particular non-English jurisdictions or taken a wider perspective. Mr M.C. Setalvad spoke for India in 1960, Professor T.B. Smith for Scotland in 1961, Dean Erwin Griswold for the United States in 1964, Lord Kilbrandon for "Other People's Law" in 1966, the Rt. Hon. O.D. Schreiner for South Africa in 1967, and the Hon. Bora Laskin for Canada in 1969. Lord Mackenzie Stuart (1977) and Lord Slynn of Hadley (1991) have contributed a European perspective. But most of my life as a Judge has been spent in small Commonwealth jurisdictions, mainly New Zealand but more recently Western Samoa and Fiji also.[2] In these it is the practice of appellate courts to look very widely for precedents. In the New Zealand Court of Appeal few significant cases would pass without consideration of at least Australian and Canadian case law, as well as United Kingdom decisions. United States cases and texts, including of course the Restatement, are consulted rather less frequently but almost invariably on novel problems in such fields as tort, contract, evidence and the Bill of Rights. In that limited respect, and only in that respect, that Court may modestly claim a necessary pre-eminence; and the habit is unlikely to be shaken off after retirement from New Zealand office.

Paradoxically, the shrinking of the jurisdiction of the Privy Council can be said to have in truth promoted the development of the common law. Seen now from a wider perspective, contributions from the various jurisdictions can be weighed according to their intrinsic merits rather than by mentally allotting them places in a hierarchy. But this process has some distance yet to go and may never be complete. An English lawyer will still tend to find the authentic voice of the common law in Reid (a Scot of course), Wilberforce or Diplock, with utterances from elsewhere of more marginal value. Similarly a Canadian lawyer might turn first to Dickson, an Australian lawyer to Dixon or Mason. (It is the

---

[1] For instance in *White v. Jones* [1995] 2 A.C. 207, to which I hope to return in the third lecture.

[2] As a result of the coups in 1987, Fiji is not at present a member of the Commonwealth, but the 1996 report of the Constitution Review Commission chaired by Sir Paul Reeves (a former Governor-General of New Zealand) hints at the prospect of readmission if a less racially-oriented Constitution is adopted. The British tradition persists in fact. It is not forgotten that Queen Victoria was elected paramount chief, Tui Viti; Queen Elizabeth II appears on banknotes; the Union Jack is part of the flag.

same with sport—asked to name the epitome of a great bowler, an Englishman might say Trueman, an Australian Lindwall, a New Zealander Hadlee.) Nevertheless it is in judicial interaction that may be seen the best prospect of continuing to evolve clear and just common-law principles for the century ahead.

Macaulay illustrated the potential longevity of the Catholic Church by imagining it "in undiminished vigour when some traveller from New Zealand shall, in the midst of a vast solitude, take his stand on a broken arch of London Bridge to sketch the ruins of St. Paul's". I do not come to sketch the metaphorical ruins of the southern end of the Palace of Westminster or the Lords of Appeal corridor within it. On the contrary, although having to own to some venturesome extra-judicial criticism of their Lordships of another day during one of the phases endemic in courts of final appeal,[3] I now recognise the privilege of taking a small part in the work of the Appellate Committee of the House and the Judicial Committee of the Privy Council during what may prove to be vintage years. Perhaps future legal historians may date an epoch from the beginning of the year 1991. Since then we have seen, to take a handful of examples, the major restitution cases of *Lipkin Gorman v. Karpnale Ltd*[4] and *Woolwich Equitable Building Society v. Inland Revenue Commissioner*[5] and the equally far-reaching tort cases of *Cambridge Water Co. v. Eastern Counties Leather Plc,*[6] *Henderson v. Merrett Syndicates Ltd*[7] and *White v. Jones.*[8] The common judicial denominator has been Lord Goff of Chieveley, now Senior Law Lord, although I must not omit to point out that the noble and learned Lord who has taken the chair this evening[9] is entitled to share in the credit as to three fifths.

The four great cases with which I have chosen to deal all happen to be ones where the House of Lords set the law of England, and consequently the law of most of the English-speaking world, on a new course by reversing decisions of the courts below. Suggested political reforms of the House usually except and preserve its

---

[3] *An Impossible Distinction* (1991) 107 L.Q.R. 46. The title was taken from the judgment of Lord Denning M.R. in *Dutton v. Bognor Regis U.D.C.* [1972] 1 Q.B. 373, 396.
[4] [1991] 2 A.C. 548
[5] [1993] A.C. 70
[6] [1994] 2 A.C. 264
[7] [1995] 2 A.C. 145
[8] [1995] 2 A.C. 207
[9] Lord Browne-Wilkinson.

judicial functions. The wisdom of doing so[10] is brought out by the four cases. For it is doubtful whether even an augmented English Court of Appeal would have been as bold at the time. Certainly the House has given some terrifying decisions over the years. Popular choices for a black list would include *Roberts v. Hopwood*,[11] *Robert Addie & Sons (Collieries) Ltd v. Dumbreck*[12] and *Chichester Diocesan Fund v. Simpson*.[13] But I believe that on the whole there is probably a credit balance.

Yet the judicial functions of the House of Lords and the Privy Council, residues of ancient constitutional legislative, executive and advisory roles which did not conform to modern theories of the separation of powers, came within an ace of extinction. The Supreme Court of Judicature Act 1873 would have abolished appeals in England to the House of Lords. Instead there was to be only a Court of Appeal, consisting of the heads of the various courts *ex officio* and Lords Justices of Appeal, with a minimum quorum of three but a discretion in "the Court" to order reargument of cases before a greater number of Judges. Provision was made as well for the Privy Council jurisdiction to be transferred to this new Court of Appeal. But practising barristers are apt to favour two tiers of appeal. That professional preference, evidenced in 1874 by the support of all the benchers of my own Inn, the Inner Temple, where this lecture is being given, harmonised with the preference of the peerage in general for the retention of their own constitutional significance. The combined force of these opinions led initially to postponements of the coming into force of the 1873 Act and ultimately to the saving of the House of Lords judicial jurisdiction, albeit with some strengthening.[14]

The Appellate Jurisdiction Act 1876, which is still in force with a few amendments, provided for appeals to the House of Lords from English, Scottish and Irish courts, to be heard by not less than three "Lords of Appeal". That term covers the Lord Chancellor; the

---

[10] Although this is not directly within the scope of the present lectures, I would add that a brief experience, as a cross-bencher, of the legislative proceedings of the House of Lords has left me convinced of both the value of the contribution of hereditary peers and the indefensibility of the power to bring in "backwoodsmen". Surely a British compromise is here waiting to be born.

[11] [1925] A.C. 578

[12] [1929] A.C. 358

[13] [1944] A.C. 341

[14] As to this paragraph, see for further particulars sections 6, 20, 21 and 53 of the Act of 1873 and Robert Stevens *Law and Politics, The House of Lords as a Judicial Body, 1800–1976*, chap. 2. There are many other scholarly writings in the field.

Lords of Appeal in Ordinary, of whom the Act of 1876 authorised for the first time the appointment of (initially) two only—the maximum number is now 12; and Peers of Parliament holding or having held "high judicial office", being broadly the office of a member of a superior British court, including a "paid Judge of the Judicial Committee of the Privy Council". The Appellate Jurisdiction Act 1887 made a change, prompted by the merits of Lord Blackburn, to the effect that a Lord of Appeal in Ordinary would be a peer for life, not merely until resignation, and another change in the dropping of "paid" from the reference to the Privy Council.[15] The second change met the circumstances of Lord Hobhouse, who had been granted an hereditary peerage but (largely for reasons of health) had never been a Judge of a United Kingdom court; furthermore, it is said that all his assiduous judicial work was done gratuitously.[16] That was a generous gift, for he delivered 200 judgments of the Privy Council, many of them in Indian cases. As it happened he sat in only three House of Lords cases, in two of which he dissented. He was noted for the tenacity of his opinions.

There is a Macaulayish nobility about the language of section 4 of the Act of 1876, which remains the foundation of the judicial responsibilities of the House of Lords, although it is not often mentioned.

"4. Form of appeal to House of Lords

Every appeal shall be brought by way of petition to the House of Lords, praying that the matter of the order or judgment appealed against may be reviewed before Her Majesty the Queen in her Court of Parliament, in order that the said Court may determine what of right, and according to the law and custom of this realm, ought to be done in the subject-matter of such appeal."

[15] One practical distinction between Lords of Appeal in Ordinary and other Lords of Appeal is that the latter (if not holding other salaried office) are piece workers, whereas the former enjoy salaries. The curious may like to know that the present lecturer's Peerage of Parliament is by appointment under the Life Peerages Act 1958 rather than the Act of 1876.

[16] Supporting evidence is supplied by a note by Lord Davey appearing in L.T. Hobhouse and J.L. Hammond *Lord Hobhouse, A Memoir* (Edward Arnold, London, 1905) 203. Before his appointment to the Judicial Committee of the Privy Council, Hobhouse served as a member of the Governor-General's Council in India, so he was a successor of Macaulay.

WHAT OF RIGHT WAS DONE FOR ARON SALOMON

Salomon was a successful leather merchant and boot manufacturer. He arranged for a limited liability company to be formed in scrupulous compliance with the formalities laid down by the Companies Act 1862, receiving 20,001 shares himself, while his wife and his five adult children subscribed for one share each. The company took over his business at a valuation probably on the high side. In return he took his shares fully paid and debentures which he mortgaged, thus enabling him to pay off existing creditors. The business was solvent at the time, but after about a year the company failed, allegedly because of strikes in the boot trade (trade unionism was becoming a power in the land). In the winding up there was a deficit in the amount needed to meet the claims of the company's unsecured creditors. A Court of Appeal of three Lords Justices, unanimously affirming the result reached by Vaughan Williams J., ordered that Salomon indemnify the company against those claims.[17]

The Court of Appeal were led by Lindley L.J., later to be a Lord of Appeal in Ordinary, whose professional reputation is thus described in Professor D.M. Walker's *Oxford Companion to Law*: "He had a very acute intellect and was very highly regarded as a judge; not least of his merits was an ability in every field of law". He was especially versed in Equity. His treatise on Partnership remains to this day the standard work.[18] Referring to the provision of the Companies Act 1862 that "Any seven or more persons associated for any lawful purpose may ... form an incorporated company with or without limited liability", Lindley said that the legislature never contemplated an extension of limited liability to sole traders or a fewer number than seven. Although there were seven members in the instant case, it was manifest that six of them were members simply in order to enable the seventh himself to carry on business with limited liability. "The object of the whole

---

[17] *Broderip v. Salomon* [1895] 2 Ch. 323

[18] In an essay entitled "Perception and Policy in Company Law Reform", published in *Corporate and Commercial Law: Modern Developments* edited by Feldman and Meisel (Lloyd's of London Press Ltd, 1996), Professor L.S. Sealy notes at pp.23–24 that Lindley's Treatise originally included the Application of the Law of Partnership to Companies, but that the work was later split into two and the Companies part is extinct. It is obviously tempting to suppose that this approach coloured Lindley's judgment in *Broderip*.

arrangement is to do the very thing which the legislature intended not to be done ...". The seven were *not* associated for a lawful purpose, but to attain a result not permitted by the Act. Going as far as to stigmatise it as a device to defraud creditors, Lindley treated the company as a trustee for Aron Salomon.

By this time Salomon's fortunes had declined to the level of pauperdom. His appeal to the House of Lords proceeded *in forma pauperis*, that is to say with waiving of counsel's fees and court costs. The Lord Chancellor was the Conservative Lord Halsbury. Although later he lent his name (for 10,000 guineas) to the incomparable encyclopaedia *Halsbury's Laws of England*, he was not a learned lawyer. At the Bar, as the late Professor Robert Heuston puts it in his *Lives of the Lord Chancellors, 1885–1940*,[19] he excelled in "plain advocacy before plain men about plain matters". Heuston goes on to classify him as one of the able men who have sat on the woolsack "who have been lawyers only so far as it was absolutely necessary". With Equity he seems to have had next to no familiarity. In *Salomon*'s case itself he was to perpetrate the howler that cestuis que trust are trustees.[20] But he compensated for this in *Salomon* by assembling to sit with him some of the intellectual judicial leaders of the day, Lords Watson, Herschell, Macnaghten and Davey, all of whom delivered speeches substantially agreeing with him in reversing the courts below.[21]

The decision of the Law Lords in *Salomon* has not had an enthusiastic academic press. Modern writers will quote Sir Otto Kahn-Freund's description of it as "calamitous".[22] When it came out (November 16, 1896) the mandarin Sir Frederick Pollock, after a tilt at the Legislature ("its usual oracular style ... leaving to the Courts the interpretation of mystic utterances"), wrote that no one who knew anything of the earlier history of the Companies Acts could doubt that such a decision as had now been given would have been impossible 30 or even 20 years previously.[23] His view was that the founders of company law legislation in using the word "associated" meant such an association as, without the help of the statute, would have made the persons members of an ordinary partnership, with unlimited personal liability.

[19] See pages 18 and 74
[20] [1897] A.C. at 30; cf. *Smith v. Cooke* [1891] A.C. 297,299.
[21] The Irish Lord of Appeal in Ordinary, Lord Morris, also sat but found it superfluous to add anything.
[22] (1944) 7 M.L.R. 54.
[23] (1897) 13 L.Q.R. 6.

Historically Pollock was no doubt right, and ethically Kahn-Freund's view has a ready appeal, albeit one-sided. But from the point of view of practical judging I think that Halsbury and his colleagues have the better of the argument. The Lord Chancellor was characteristically cutting—

> "Lopes L.J. says: 'The Act contemplated the incorporation of seven independent bona fide members, who had a mind and will of their own, and were not the mere puppets of an individual who, adopting the machinery of the Act, carried on his old business in the same way as before, when he was a sole trader'. The words 'seven independent bona fide members with a mind and a will of their own, and not the puppets of an individual', are by construction to be read into the Act. Lopes L.J. also said that the company was a mere nominis umbra."

Without applauding the sarcasm, one can see the validity of the point. It is the kind of point that can trouble a working Judge, however bent on giving the words of the Act a purposive construction (in the current phraseology), "such fair, large, and liberal construction and interpretation as will best ensure the attainment of the object of the Act ... according to its true intent, meaning and spirit" (in the periphrasis of the New Zealand Acts Interpretation Act 1924[24]).

However laudable purposive interpretation may be, a practical Judge must also recognise its limitations. Lord Simonds will be legally immortal for his chiselled rebuke that the approach of Lord Denning (as he was to become) to filling gaps in statutes was "a naked usurpation of the legislative function under the thin disguise of interpretation".[25] I prefer, as in substance did Lord Radcliffe in his tactfully-worded dissent in that case, Lord Denning's determination to find out the intention of Parliament rather than subjecting an Act to destructive analysis. Nor should any apology

---

[24] Section 5(j). The value of this exhortation, as furnishing the courts with an additional instrument to achieve justice, was perhaps underrated by the English Court of Appeal, admittedly under the undue influence of expert evidence from a New Zealand barrister, in *Attorney-General of New Zealand v. Ortiz* [1984] A.C. 1, 29. The provision was touched on lightly only in the House of Lords in the same case, *ibid.* 49. The actual decision in that case, that to cause an unlawfully exported historic article to be forfeited to the Crown it had to be seized before the export, largely nullified the statute providing for forfeiture. It was an instance of the smuggling of an antiquity and later auction at Sotherby's in London.

[25] *Magor & St Mellons Rural District Council v. Newport Corporation* [1952] A.C. 189, 191.

9

be needed, although I fear that too often in the present era one is expected, for being guided by the great jurist. But there remains a part of the Simonds condemnation which has real force. I tried to express this in a New Zealand case by saying that the courts can in a sense fill gaps in an Act, but only in order to make the Act work as Parliament must have intended.[26] My friend Sir Anthony Mason, with whom I have the pleasure of sitting in the Supreme Court of Fiji, has expressed in fuller language much the same idea in the High Court of Australia.[27] He has held that the justification for departing from the literal rule is not confined to results that can be labelled "absurd" or the like. It extends, he says, to any situation in which for good reason the operation of the statute on a literal reading does not conform to the legislative intent as ascertained from the provisions of the statute, *including the policy which may be discerned from those provisions.*

My colleagues and I have recently applied these ideas in Western Samoa. In that small island jurisdiction, the issue was whether a successful candidate in a parliamentary election, resigning on the eve of an inevitable decision against him on an election petition alleging corrupt practice, could ensure that a new electoral roll was used for the by-election (as normal in by-elections) rather than the old roll (as required for by-elections resulting from findings of corrupt practice). It was easy to see that the eleventh hour resignation could defeat the statutory intent; but the difficulties in formulating a workable alternative rule were thought by the court to go too far in the direction of requiring policy-making rather than interpretation.[28] Thus has Lord Simonds been to some extent vindicated in the South Seas. Thus, too, was Lord Halsbury's *Salomon* reasoning reflected in a wholly different context. In terms of the *Salomon* context, once an inquiry is admitted into where lies the beneficial ownership or control of company shares, the difficulty of inferring workable limits to the statutory right of incorporation with limited liability becomes practically insuper-

---

[26] *Northland Milk Vendors Association v. Northern Milk Ltd* [1988] 1 N.Z.L.R. 530. The court was able there to infer from the scheme and purpose of the Act, rather than its actual language, that home deliveries of milk had to continue, pending the promulgation of a new licensing system, notwithstanding an apparent interregnum of no control and alleged common law freedom to trade without control. An implied contract to that effect was held to arise between the existing vendors and the new concessionaire.

[27] In a joint judgment with Wilson J. in *Cooper Brookes (Woollongong) Pty Ltd v. Federal Commissioner of Taxation* (1981) 147 C.L.R. 297, 320–323.

[28] *Chief Electoral Officer v. Samoa All People's Party,* September 1996.

10

able. Any policy beyond the literal terms of the Act has to be largely arbitrary, and the legislature has not exercised its right to make the choice.

So, one hundred years later, one can find irresistible force in Lord Halsbury's summation—

> "My Lords, the learned judges appear to me not to have been absolutely certain in their own minds whether to treat the company as a real thing or not. If it was a real thing; if it had a legal existence, and if consequently the law attributed to it certain rights and liabilities in its constitution as a company, it appears to me to follow as a consequence that it is impossible to deny the validity of the transactions into which it has entered".

THE GLOBAL CONSEQUENCES OF *SALOMON*

It is no exaggeration to put the effects of the House of Lords speeches in *Salomon*'s case under the above heading. As Professor L.C.B. Gower says in the leading scholarly general work on Company Law,[29] "Unquestionably the limited liability company has been a major instrument in making possible the industrial and commercial developments which have occurred throughout the world." Essentially this is due to the insistence of Lord Halsbury and his colleagues that such a company has an identity wholly separate from that of its members. The resulting potential for attracting and amassing the contributions of relatively small investors is obvious. The family or one-man company, as in *Salomon* itself, has achieved immense popularity and respectability, even though its advantages are diminished by the practice of major lenders, such as banks, insisting on personal guarantees— the efficacy of which were much tested in the flood of litigation following the stock market crash of October 1987, with the search (commonly fruitless) for technical loopholes to avoid liability.

Moreover, companies can hold shares in and control other companies, so in dealings not at arm's length it is possible by techniques such as transfer pricing to ensure, subject to legislation to the contrary, that earnings within a group of companies constituting in reality one economic entity are distributed so as to minimise tax.

---

[29] Gower, *Principles of Modern Company Law* (5th ed. 1992) p. 70.

11

Avoidance or evasion (terms which do not fall, I think, into readily distinct categories) of local taxation regimes or legislative controls must be indeed among the primary reasons for the international proliferation of companies. There is a vast literature. Professor John Prebble of the Victoria University of Wellington promotes the term *ectopia* to bring out that concepts used in the imposition of taxes, such as income and the place and time of its derivation, are unnatural and dislocated from the facts to which they relate; he also calls them fictional characteristics.[30] He has persuaded me that there is a good deal in this thesis, but, whether or not his terminology takes on, it is plain that subsidiary companies and inter-company shareholdings have been key elements in the rise of the multi-nationals, some of which are now perhaps better called supra-nationals.

Lord Halsbury's "real thing" is of course often regarded as a misnomer. Incorporated companies are seen as notional constructs, abstractions,[31] existing in minds and on paper. They are easily created. In London, Companies House provides a same-day incorporation service, taking only a few hours, for £200. For a normal formation taking a week to ten days the fee is £20. Companies House is an Executive Agency of the Department of Trade and Industry, and may be on the way to becoming a company itself. Its Annual Report for 1995–1996 records that 147,000 new companies were incorporated during the year and that the average live register stood at 1.05 million companies. A leading firm of commercial solicitors, such as Linklaters & Paines of London[32] and nine other capitals, will itself form twelve shelf companies a month to provide a swift and comprehensive service to clients on demand. Some will be private limited companies with an authorised share capital of £100 and an issued capital of one £1 share. For since 1992 it has been possible to register a single member private company.[33] Although driven by a European

---

[30] He will forgive me for noting that one of his best expositions of his thesis is entitled *Philosophical and Design Problems that arise from the Ectopic Nature of Income Tax Law and their Impact on the Taxation of International Trade and Instruments.* Those of the Common People of the United Kingdom who are able to do so may find it in (1994–95) 13 Chinese Yearbook of International Law and Affairs 111.

[31] *Lennard's Carrying Co. Ltd v. Asiatic Petroleum Co. Ltd* [1915] A.C. 705,714, per Viscount Haldane, L.C.

[32] I am grateful to their London Manager, Company Secretarial, for much of the information in the text.

[33] See 7(1) *Halsbury's Laws of England*, (4th ed.) 1996 Reissue, para.81; Companies Act 1985, s.1(3A).

Directive[34] (like some other changes in English company law) this is the logical apogee of the concept that guided Aron Salomon's more complicated and more expensive steps. The companies that are not private will be public limited companies with an authorised share capital of £50,000 (all of which must be allotted before a trading certificate can be obtained) and two issued £1 shares. The company, the services of other companies which will act as nominee directors or secretaries, the memorandum of association and other documentation can be sold to the client virtually instantly. Less up-market incorporation agents will supply their customers with blank registers and forms and perhaps a simple set of post-incorporation outline minutes. The customers are then left to do the post-incorporation work themselves.

GETTING ROUND *SALOMON*

In the main the concept that a duly incorporated limited liability company, if not a real thing, is at least not to be identified with its shareholders has been faithfully followed by British and other Commonwealth courts ever since *Salomon*'s case. But there has been some gnawing away at the edges of doctrine, a process commonly described as piercing or lifting the corporate veil. I believe that there is only one broad class of cases where this is truly consistent with the *Salomon* reasoning. They are all cases where, under enactments such as those against fraudulent or wrongful trading, or on the permissible interpretation of an enactment or contract, or for the purposes of common law or equitable principles against fraud or oppression or relating to agency, it is necessary to look at what has happened in fact rather than form.[35]

---

[34] The Twelfth of the EEC Company Law Directives. The relevant subsection is inserted into the Companies Act by the Companies (Single Member Private Limited Companies) Regulations 1992 (S.I. 1992 No.1699) made under the European Communities Act 1972, s.2(2). Thus United Kingdom membership of the European Community enables a Minister of the Crown to alter an Act of the United Kingdom Parliament.

[35] For a convenient up-to-date summary of the English case law, see *Halsbury, op.cit.* paragraphs 93 and 94. A useful recent illustration is *Nicholas v. Soundcraft Electronics Ltd* [1993] B.C.L.C. 300, C.A., where it was accepted that a holding company may conduct the affairs of a subsidiary in a manner unfairly prejudicial to a member of the subsidiary, thus enabling the latter to apply for statutory relief. The leading case to the same effect is *Scottish Co-operative Wholesale Society Ltd v. Meyer* [1959] A.C. 324. While there was reference in *Soundcraft* to the reality of one economic unit, the separate existence of the two companies is fully consistent with the decision and in a sense its basis.

Admittedly it is not always easy to determine whether a case falls within that broad class. But uncertainty in borderline cases is inherent in the law. It is a large part of the reason why there have to be Judges—a fact not grappled with by hard right academic writers who impliedly claim that legitimate Judge-made law ceased growing at some unspecified date and place.

So, in *Lee v. Lee's Air Farming Ltd*,[36] an aerial top-dressing pilot, killed in a crash during those hazardous operations, owned effectively a one-man company. By the articles he was governing director for life. He had appointed himself the company's only pilot. A Court of Appeal which would be regarded in New Zealand as strong (Gresson P., North and Cleary JJ.) held that his widow's claim to workers' compensation failed because giving orders and receiving orders were incompatible functions. Therefore the relationship of master and servant had not been created. The Privy Council (Viscount Simonds, Lords Reid, Tucker, Denning and Morris of Borth-y-Gest) reversed this decision on an orthodox *Salomon* approach:[37] they were separate legal entities so as to enable the company to give orders to the deceased. Sir Alfred North wrote in his privately published *Reminiscences* that the appeal was allowed "on a very narrow and controversial point".

Perhaps so. Certainly it was not an easy issue. But, were the same question to arise today, it might be solved by a more overt invocation of the policy of the Workers' Compensation Act; in fact it does not now arise, as New Zealand has a more comprehensive accident compensation scheme. In substance the old Act provided, for workers and their dependants, insured compensation for work-related accidents. Nothing in the scheme or purpose of the Act justified excluding the deceased and his family from the statutory protection. On this view the case did not fall within the broad class of exceptions to *Salomon* which I have mentioned. The point is that a company duly incorporated under the Companies Act must always be treated, in accordance with *Salomon*, as a legal person separate and distinct from its shareholders. Only when some other statute, contract or doctrine is wide enough to embrace that separate and distinct legal person may the consequences of *Salomon* become unimportant in fact. In the eye of the law,

[36] [1959] N.Z.L.R. 393.
[37] [1961] A.C. 12.

14

however, the difference between the company and its shareholders remains absolute.[38]

THE SHAM DOCTRINE

It is received doctrine that there is a second broad class of cases in which the *Salomon* principle is displaced, namely cases where the corporate veil is "a mere façade concealing the true facts". In a Scottish case in 1978[39] the House of Lords paid lip-service to the existence of such a doctrine, applicable in special circumstances, but only to reject it on the facts of that case. I doubt very much whether it really does exist. It is a version of the concept of sham, which has an insidious appeal to Judges and other lawyers but is often itself a spurious concept. As Diplock L.J. (as he then was) once said "... for acts or documents to be a 'sham', with whatever legal consequences follow from this, all the parties thereto must have a common intention that the acts or documents are not to create the legal rights and obligations which they give the appearance of creating."[40] Not uncommonly parties enter deliberately into transactions knowing that the efficacy in law of the form adopted is essential to achieve their purposes, yet later one party

[38] This proposition does not derogate from the principle, touched on later in this lecture, that some acts of shareholders will be attributed to the company. Similarly the nationality of the directors and shareholders may give a company the character of an alien enemy: *Daimler Company Ltd v. Continental Tyre & Rubber Co. (Great Britain) Ltd* [1916] 2 A.C. 307. The Earl of Halsbury's vigorous language at 316 need not be seen as inconsistent with what he said in *Salomon*. Public policy may require that a company in alien ownership and control be itself treated as an alien. Contrast the South African case of *Dadoo Ltd v. Krugersdorf Municipal Council* 1920 A.D. 530, from which an extract appears in Professor Harry Rajak's *Sourcebook of Company Law* (2nd ed. Jordans, Bristol) 1995, pp. 98–100.

[39] *Woolfson v. Strathclyde Regional Council* 1978 S.L.T. 159, 161, per Lord Keith of Kinkel.

[40] *Snook v. London and West Riding Investments Ltd* [1967] 2 Q.B. 786, 802. An impeccable application of this analysis appears to be *Hilton v. Plustitle Ltd* [1989] 1 W.L.R. 149. A landlord's advertised policy was to let flats only to limited companies; he wished thereby to avoid the Rent Acts. To comply with his policy a would-be occupant bought a shelf company for £150, signing the tenancy agreement as managing director of the company. She occupied the flat as nominee of her company. Her brother guaranteed the rent. After the expiration of the tenancy the landlord was held entitled to an order for possession: the company was in truth the intended tenant and did not enjoy statutory protection. Gower, *op.cit.*, 133, n.60, suggests that the decision is inconsistent with *Antoniades v. Villiers* [1990] 1 A.C. 417, but in the latter case it was never intended by the parties that the agreement should operate in accordance with its terms.

or both may claim, spuriously, that the legal form was a façade.[41] To let in the concept of sham then would be loose thinking, but it can be a temptation, unless recognised for what it is.

In the leading modern English case, *Adams v. Cape Industries PLC*,[42] Cape, an English company was the parent of an international group concerned with the mining of asbestos in South Africa and its sale in various countries. Asbestos mined by one of the subsidiary companies was sold by another subsidiary company for use in a Texas factory. Workers sued in Texas for damages for disease alleged to have been caused by the factory dust. Cape was named as first defendant, and a default judgment was obtained against it. Whether the judgment would be enforced in England was held to turn (apart from an issue of natural justice, outside the present discussion) on whether Cape was present in the United States. Presence was held to turn on whether one or other of two successive Illinois companies, which acted as marketing agents for the group but did not make contracts on behalf of Cape, were at least in part carrying on the business of Cape. In judgments of extraordinary length[43] (the report occupies some 150 pages) Scott J. and the Court of Appeal (Slade, Mustill and Ralph Gibson L.JJ.) held not.

So far the case may be seen as a straightforward application of *Salomon*. Save in an unacceptably loose sense, even the first Illinois company, although a wholly-owned subsidiary, was not carrying on the business of Cape. There was nothing in the principles of English private international law governing the question which national courts have jurisdiction over a tort case of this kind to require the business of a subsidiary to be treated as partly the business of its parent. But the two English Courts had to grapple also with an argument of façade or sham. This they likewise

---

[41] For instance, in *Mills v. Dowdall* [1983] N.Z.L.R. 154, to avoid estate and gift duties a property was transferred from mother to son at full value, but it was planned that the debt for the price would be written off progressively. It was of course held that this was not a gift of the property.

[42] [1990] Ch. 433.

[43] Some idea of the practical impossibility that the courts would face if they set out to cover everything which textbook or academic writers would like to see discussed may be gained by noting that, while describing the *Cape* judgment as mammoth, Professor Gower would have it even longer: *op.cit.* 130. This is a tribute to both his modesty and the Court of Appeal's authority. It has been suggested that the Appeal Committee of the House of Lords was wrong to refuse leave to appeal, as it did, in *Cape* (see [1990] Ch. at 572); but there were probably too many hurdles in the way of a successful appeal.

rejected.[44] Cape was in law entitled to organise the group's affairs so as to have the practical benefit of the group's asbestos trade in the United States without the risks of tortious liability there. Any argument to the contrary could only be based on public policy, and English private international law does not go so far.

The dictum in *Woolfson v. Strathclyde Regional Council* already quoted led the Court of Appeal in *Cape* to describe the "mere façade" exception as well-recognised.[45] But they admitted to finding rather sparse guidance as to when the exception would apply. For an example they virtually fell back on a first instance judgment of Russell J. in the Chancery Division, *Jones v. Lipman*.[46] There a vendor, in order to avoid being compelled to complete a contract for the sale of land, formed a company, his solicitor's clerk being the only other shareholder, and transferred the land to it. Since the company was in the vendor's control, there was no difficulty in granting a decree of specific performance against him. Describing the company as a creation of the vendor, a device, sham and mask, the Judge also decreed specific performance directly against it. Those epithets, however, do not appear to have been needed to justify the remedy. No particular difficulty should arise in holding that a company or any other purchaser acquiring property with actual notice that the transaction is a fraud on a prior purchaser takes subject to the latter's equity. In truth the very granting of the remedy against the company brings out that it was *not* a sham.

In sum I respectfully submit to the Common People of the United Kingdom and their Judges that, on a true analysis, the so-called "sham" or "façade" exception to *Salomon* is unneeded and unsound. After a century the principle of *Salomon* has and should have a vigour as undiminished as Macaulay's Catholic Church. It rightly remains the key principle of company law. Its limits are marked not by the doctrine of sham, but by the proper scope of other principles, such as the public policy exemplified by the *Daimler* case.[47]

---

[44] Apart from an immaterial exception. The Court of Appeal were prepared to treat a Liechtenstein subsidiary as a façade, but as that subsidiary carried on no business in the United States the issue was seen as irrelevant.

[45] [1990] Ch. at 539

[46] [1962] 1 W.L.R. 832; [1962] 1 All E.R. 442. Russell J. Followed *Gilford Motor Co. Ltd v. Horne* [1933] Ch. 935, C.A., to which the comments in the text must also apply.

[47] *Supra*, n.38.

TAKING *SALOMON* FURTHER

Contrary to what is sometimes seen as the tendency, the *Salomon* principle may wax rather than wane. It is convenient to repeat here something that I put before an Oxford audience in 1993,[48] not for its own sake but to introduce its aftermath. In *Trevor Ivory Ltd v. Anderson*,[49] the New Zealand Court of Appeal was concerned with negligent advice about spraying, given by a one-man company to a commercial fruit grower, the spray having killed the plaintiff's raspberry crop as well as the weeds. The company was held liable in contract and tort.[50] The issue of present relevance was whether the owner of the company was personally liable in tort as well. The Court held not. Although it was his reputed expertise as an agricultural consultant that had led the plaintiff to contract with his company, he had made it clear, by forming the company and trading as the company, that the business was being carried on with limited liability. He had assumed no extra personal duty.[51]

That decision has no attraction at first sight for lawyers brought up on the premise that the liability of a company or other employer for acts of its or his principal or other employee is vicarious in the sense of being liability for a tort committed by a servant or agent in the course of employment. The decision was duly assailed on that ground by a lecturer at the University of Canterbury (New Zealand), Mr D. A. Wishart, in an article entitled *Anthropomorphism Rampant*.[52] He thought that the Court had not considered the issue in sufficient depth. It is agreeable to record that, after crossing the Tasman to La Trobe University and reading the Oxford paper, Mr Wishart wrote to me apologising in some measure. He now accepted that there had been "profound thought" in the Court of Appeal, while admitting to doubts about the com-

---

[48] In *The Frontiers of Liability*, Vol.2, 1994, papers presented at a series of seminars of the Society of Public Teachers of Law, edited by Professor Peter Birks. This paper was on *The Condition of the Law of Tort* and the relevant passage is at p.57.

[49] [1992] 2 N.Z.L.R. 517

[50] This was before the House of Lords also came to accept concurrent sources of duty in *Henderson v. Merrett Syndicates Ltd* [1995] 2 A.C. 145, a subject to which I hope to return in the third lecture of the present series.

[51] If the plaintiff had reasonably thought that it was dealing with an individual, the result might have been different, as pointed out in Ford and Austin, *Principles of Corporation Law*, (7th ed., Sydney 1995), 588

[52] [1993] N.Z.L.J. 175.

partmentalisation of law—doubts which we lawyers all share. Such is the generosity of scholarship.

I shall attempt similar generosity by saying that at the time of the *Trevor Ivory* judgment I was unaware that less than two months previously the Supreme Court of Canada had instructively adjudicated on a wider issue in *London Drugs Ltd v. Kuehne & Nagel International Ltd*.[53] In that case employees of a corporate defendant, a warehouseman, had negligently damaged the plaintiff's transformer. The company was held liable in bailment, contract and negligence, but its liability was limited to $40 by a clause in the contract. The issue was the liability or otherwise of the individual employees. Five members of the Supreme Court of Canada held that they were personally liable but to the extent of $40 only, four of these Judges taking the ground that the employees were third-party beneficiaries of the limitation clause, the other using the tort principle of acceptance of risk. Their judgments are of value on the question of limitation of third-party liability.[54] What is of more present interest, however, is the far-ranging and brilliant judgment of La Forest J., who held that the employees were not liable to the plaintiff at all.

One cannot do justice to that judgment in a few minutes in a lecture. The best that one can do is to stand back and record some outstanding impressions. La Forest's theme is that tort liability related to the performance of a contract must be determined with an eye to the contractual context. The question becomes whether in that setting the plaintiff has reasonably relied on the answerability of individual employees. An employer, including a company, may be vicariously liable for the negligence of the employees, even though they are immune from suit[55] by the plaintiffs. In this instance any such reliance would not have been reasonable. It was a planned transaction in which the plaintiff had chosen to deal with a company: the plaintiff and the company could allocate risks between them and take out appropriate insurance, whereas in practice the individual employees did not have the same opportunity: the case concerned property damage and

[53] [1992] 3 S.C.R.299; 97 D.L.R. (4th) 261
[54] The latest authoritative English judgment on this subject is *The Mahkutai* [1996] 3 W.L.R. 1; [1996] 3 All E.R. 502, P.C.
[55] This is reminiscent of *Broom v. Morgan* [1953] 1 Q.B. 597, C.A., where, in the days when spouses could not sue each other in tort, a wife was held nevertheless entitled to recover from the employer of the husband for the latter's negligence in the course of employment.

economic loss only, there being no overriding considerations relating to personal safety: it was not a case of reliance on the specialised skills of an individual employee: the natural hope of customers that "employees of their co-contractant will do the job right" is not enough to fasten liability on them for non-intentional torts.

London Drugs is the subject of much academic debate. But the writers have concentrated mainly on its bearing on general issues of vicarious liability or privity of contract, rather than the specifically corporate law aspect.[56] For our more limited purpose, however, La Forest J. has made a particularly constructive contribution. Declining to express an opinion on whether a British Columbia case[57] on which the New Zealand Court had partly relied in *Trevor Ivory* is of general application, he notes that, both with one-man companies and with companies providing for their clients the services of professional or other skilled employees, there arise issues as to the tort liability of the individuals which can be distinguished from the general run of vicarious liability cases. But I understand him to lean towards his solution of no individual liability in property or economic loss cases in those special categories also; provided in the first category that the principal employee has at least drawn the attention of the client to the fact that he desires to take advantage of the corporate vehicle to limit his personal liability.[58] In *Trevor Ivory* the New Zealand Court held that impliedly that had been done. In *London Drugs* itself, La Forest J. said[59]—

"The question of reliance on a particular individual in such cases may give rise to difficulties because it may be the reputation of one person that attracts work to a firm while others may end up doing the work. It is particularly important in cases involving professionals to distinguish between mere reliance in fact and *reasonable* reliance on the employee's pocketbook. Unlike this case, in which it clearly makes no sense to impose upon the employee an obligation to insure against property

[56] To mention only a handful of discussions, Professor George Curtis anticipated some of La Forest J.'s ideas fifty years ago in an article in (1936) 14 C.B.R. 725. Marvin G. Baer has written an extensive case note in (1993) 72 C.B.R. 385 in which he disagrees in one way or another with all the judgments in *London Drugs* but criticises La Forest J. less than the other members of the Supreme Court. In (1993) 109 L.Q.R. 349, Professor Stephen Waddams sees the significance of the case in terms of the relaxation of the privity of contract rule.

[57] *Sealand of the Pacific v. Robert C McHaffie Ltd* (1974) 51 D.L.R. (3d) 702.

[58] [1992] 3 S.C.R. at 386.

[59] *Ibid.* 387.

loss, such cases raise with particular acuity the question of whether in effect requiring double insurance by both the firm and the employee makes sense in that context. Ultimately the question of reasonableness of the plaintiff's reliance may depend essentially on the answer to that question. Such an approach would avoid difficult definitional questions concerning whether a particular employee is 'skilled' or a 'professional'."

More recently he returned to the theme in *Edgeworth Construction Ltd v. N D Lea & Associates Ltd.*[60] The successful bidder for a road building contract with a province had allegedly lost money because of errors in the specifications and drawings prepared for the province by an engineering company. The Supreme Court held that the contractor had a *prima facie* cause of action against the engineering company for negligent misrepresentation.[61] As against the individual engineers, though, all the Judges considered that by affixing their professional seals to the drawings they did not assume a duty of care to the contractor. Concurring in a judgment delivered by McLachlin J., La Forest J. said[62]—

"The situation of the individual engineers is quite different. While they may, in one sense, have expected that persons in the position of the appellant would rely on their work, they would expect that the appellant would place reliance on their firm's pocketbook and not theirs for indemnification; see *London Drugs, supra,* at pp.386–87. Looked at the other way, the appellant could not reasonably rely for indemnification on the individual engineers. It would have to show that it was relying on the particular expertise of an individual engineer without regard to the corporate character of the engineering firm. It would seem quite unrealistic, as my colleague observes, to hold that the mere presence of an individual engineer's seal was sufficient indication of personal reliance (or for that matter voluntary assumption of risk). In considering the matter, other more general policy issues should be considered. As I noted in *London Drugs, supra,* at p.387, the case raises with particular acuity the question of whether in effect requiring double insurance by both the firm and the employee makes sense in that context."

Not motivated by *Salomon*, these observations from the rich field of modern Canadian jurisprudence are nevertheless in complete harmony with *Salomon*. As to property damage or other economic

---

[60] [1993] 3 S.C.R. 206.
[61] An application of the *Hedley Byrne* principle, to be discussed in the third of these lectures.
[62] [1993] 3 S.C.R. at 212.

loss caused by the activities of a limited liability company, those who have sufficiently manifested an intention to carry on business with limited liability should not have to insure themselves personally as well. I do not profess to be an economist and believe that Judges are usually well advised to steer clear of the clashes of economic dogmas.[63] But it seems conceivable that in this field *Salomon* makes good economics as well as good sense and good law.

ATTRIBUTION

The argument so far has been that, as a corollary of *Salomon*, a duly incorporated company can never be a sham. Moreover the general effect of the Companies Act 1985, section 13, is that an unrevoked certificate of registration is conclusive evidence of due incorporation. Section 13(4) declares that from the certified date of incorporation the body corporate is capable of exercising all the functions of an incorporated company.[64] What these are is not specified in the Companies Act apart from a reference in section 1(1) to "a lawful purpose". The field is wide open.

Many of us were brought up in the law in an era when the *ultra vires* doctrine, derived from limitations on a company's objects inferred from its memorandum of association, was of quite considerable moment as regards at least matters of property and contract; but now, except in internal issues as to the duties of directors, *ultra vires* has largely lost its sting in company law. Thus, by sections 3A, 35A and 35B of the 1985 Act, the validity of an act done by a company shall not be called into question on the ground of lack of capacity by reason of anything in the company's memorandum: in favour of a person dealing with a company in good faith, the powers of the board of directors to bind the company, or

---

[63] Judge Richard Posner, a most distinguished representative in the law of the Chicago school of economists, has described the dissenting judgment of Holmes J. in *Lochner v. New York* 198 U.S. 45 (1905) as the greatest judicial opinion of the last hundred years. The judgment occupies less than two pages. It holds that the United States constitution does not embody a particular economic theory, whether of paternalism or of *laissez-faire*, and that a limitation of working hours in bakeries to 60 a week and 10 a day could be regarded by a reasonable man as proper on the score of health. I am indebted to Professor Basil Markesinis in his most recent inaugural lecture for this reference to Posner. See "The Comparative (or a plea for broader legal education)" in *Presiding Problems in the Law* P.B.H. Birks ed. (Oxford 1996) 116, n. 77.

[64] In the case of a public company a further certificate is required regarding share capital requirements.

authorise others to do so, shall be deemed to be free of any limitation under the company's constitution: parties to transactions with the company are not bound to enquire as to whether it is permitted by the memorandum or as to any limitation on the power of the directors: where the memorandum states that the object of the company is to carry on business as a general commercial company, the object is to carry on any trade or business whatsoever and all things incidental or conducive thereto. Cautious solicitors still include, though, clauses going beyond commerce in a narrow sense and clearly allowing philanthropy.

Neither the statutory limitation to "a lawful purpose" nor the *ultra vires* doctrine is held to prevent a company from committing a crime or a tort. For these purposes the concepts of vicarious liability and identification are used. I shall turn to them shortly. First a few words should be said about the received proposition that an artificial person such as a company incorporated under the Companies Act cannot do everything that a natural person can do. One can perhaps safely say, for instance, that at present it cannot marry, have children, vote at a parliamentary election, become a Member of Parliament or a peer, commit murder or rape, be appointed a Judge or a professor, or be called as a barrister.

There is no inherent reason, however, why the identification concept cannot be extended to at least some of these cases also. After all, only in recent years the carefully considered ruling of Turner J. in *R. v. P & O European Ferries (Dover) Ltd*[65] held for virtually the first time that by the common law of England a company could be guilty of manslaughter.[66] The basic reason why the concept has not been carried further is that corporate liability has been perceived to be incongruous in the light of the public policy reflected in the relevant substantive rules of common or statute law. The law aims to approximate to reality as generally understood. As Lord Blackburn put it in *Pharmaceutical Society v. London & Provincial Supply Association Ltd*,[67] "Nobody in common talk if he were asked, Who is the richest person in London, would

---

[65] (1990) 93 Cr. App. R. 72.

[66] The Judge was able to cite dicta in favour of his ruling, which somewhat surprisingly is described in Archbold 1995, para. 1–83, as of persuasive authority only. He did not follow the New Zealand Court of Appeal in *R. v. Murray Wright Ltd* [1970] N.Z.L.R. 476, who had based their decision to the contrary on the statutory definition of homicide as the killing of one human being by another. Both the concept of identification and the concept of vicarious liability do seem capable of overcoming this point.

[67] (1880) 5 App. Cas. 857,869

23

answer, The London and North-Western Railway Company. The thing is absurd." A subsidiary reason advanced is that some crimes can only be punished corporeally, but this does not explain why the company cannot be *convicted* of murder.

It will not do to underestimate the strength of some of these public policy considerations. Even Professor Gower seems to fall into a Homeric nod when he says of the rule that a company cannot conduct a court action in person that it "appears to serve no purpose other than to protect the monopoly of the legal profession".[68] That view is echoed even more trenchantly by Professor Sealy in an instructive essay which I have already cited.[69] But what led the New Zealand Court of Appeal in recent times to reject that view and reaffirm the rule as generally applicable (subject to the inherent discretion of the court to hear any representative in particular cases) was not any desire to protect the Bar but the all-too-real risk of allowing scope for irresponsible advocacy.[70]

Delivering the judgment of the Privy Council in *Meridian Global Funds Management Asia Ltd v. Securities Commission*,[71] Lord Hoffmann has said:

> "'It is worth pausing at this stage to make what may seem an obvious point. Any statement about what a company has or has not done, or can or cannot do, is necessarily a reference to the rules of attribution (primary and general) as they apply to that company. Judges sometimes say that a company "as such" cannot do anything; it must act by servants or agents. This may seem an unexceptionable, even banal remark. And of course the meaning is usually perfectly clear. But a reference to a company "as such" might suggest that there is something out there called the company of which one can meaningfully say that it can or cannot do something. There is in fact no such thing as the company as such, no Ding an sich, only the applicable rules. To say that a company cannot do something means only that there is no one whose doing of that act would, under the applicable rules of attribution, count as an act of the company."

Decisions of the board of directors or by unanimous or sufficient assent of the shareholders are prime examples of what will normally be attributed to a company. In going further the courts have commonly used one or other of the two concepts already mentioned, namely vicarious liability and identification. True

---

[68] Op.cit.n. 27 *supra*, at 195.
[69] *Supra* n.16, at 18–19
[70] *Re G J Mannix Ltd* [1984] 1 N.Z.L.R. 309
[71] [1995] 2 A.C. 500, 506–507.

vicarious liability has in the main presented no particular problem. The actions of an employee in the course of his or her employment, or of an agent within the scope of his or her authority, are attributed to the company as to any other principal. One curious problem has been thrown up, however, by the judgment of the Privy Council in *Kuwait Asia Bank E.C. v. National Mutual Life Nominees Ltd.*[72] It appears to have been held that two full-time employees of a bank who were appointed by their employer to act as directors of a company in which it held shares were not acting in the course of their employment while they acted as directors. It may be said, albeit contrary to commercial reality, that in their capacity as directors they were bound to ignore the interests and wishes of their employer; but conflicts of interest, and even fraud, are not usually thought to exclude vicarious liability in questions with third parties. The law requires an employed driver to ignore the employer's instructions to drive at a speed dangerous to other road users; nevertheless by complying with the law he will not take himself outside the course of his employment. And the judgment does expose the wider problem that, insofar as they insist that nominee directors must refrain from protecting and furthering the interests of the appointors, they fly in the face of the very raison d'être of the power to appoint.

Identification is a different concept, classically based on Viscount Haldane Lord Chancellor's description in the *Lennard's* case[73] "... really the directing mind and will of the corporation, the very ego and centre of the personality of the corporation." In the *Meridian* case the New Zealand Court of Appeal applied this concept to hold that the company knew that it had acquired a substantial interest in a public issuer (and therefore became bound by securities legislation to give certain notices) when its chief investment officer improperly bought in the name of the company certain shares for $21 million.[74] Hardie Boys J., who delivered the judgment, carefully explained, citing a collection of authorities from various jurisdictions, that the doctrine had been held to extend to a directing mind and will *in a particular area of responsibility: there need not be a delegation of all the company's powers.* The account of the Court of Appeal judgment given in the Privy Council judgment says simply[75] that the Court decided that the

[72] [1991] 1 A.C. 187.
[73] [1915] A.C. 705, 713.
[74] [1994] 2 N.Z.L.R. 291, 302.
[75] [1995] 2 A.C. at 505.

chief investment officer's knowledge should be attributed to Meridian because he was the "directing mind and will of the company", omitting the qualifications which I have just stressed and so conveying the impression that the judgment was more foolish than it might otherwise have seemed. But is not to be thought that there was any mens rea in this omission. Undoubtedly it will have arisen from an aim at economy in a summary.

Their Lordships went on to explain that there has been some misunderstanding of the true principle on which *Lennard*'s case was decided. They held that in every case the rule of attribution to be applied depends on the particular statutory context. They guarded themselves against being understood to mean that whenever a servant of a company has authority to do an act on its behalf, knowledge of that act will be for all purposes attributed to the company. In the case of a corporate security holder that which should count as the knowledge of the company was the knowledge of the person who, with the authority of the company, acquired the relevant interest, "the person who had authority to do the deal".[76] But they did not expressly say that an investment manager with authority to spend $21 million or more in buying shares at his discretion was not, in that sector of the company's activities, its directing mind and will. The value of the Privy Council's refinement of the concept of identification may well be considerable but remains to be demonstrated by future cases.

The actual decision in the *Meridian* case was never very difficult. The same result was reached at all three curial levels. What drove the company to go as far as the Privy Council was the concern of its parent company that a finding of breach of securities legislation was standing on the record against the subsidiary. This underlines that a company, once it has left any shelf, may acquire a character and a reputation. Although Lord Reid said "A company cannot be injured in its feelings, it can only be injured in its pocket",[77] nineteenth century dicta restricting the kinds of cases in which it can sue in defamation[78] have now to be viewed with caution. That a company, as distinct from a local authority,[79] can sue in defamation in at least some cases seems to be well settled.

For, on balance, legislatures and courts have carried the *Salomon* principle of separate identity to ever greater lengths. Logical

---

[76] *Ibid.* at 511
[77] *Lewis v. Daily Telegraph Ltd* [1964] A.C. 234,262.
[78] See 28 Halsbury's Laws of England, 4th ed. para.25.
[79] *Derbyshire County Council v. Times Newspapers Ltd* [1993] A.C. 534.

analysis may justify a denial that there is something out there called the company of which one can meaningfully say that it can or cannot do something; but we have long been told what the life of the law is, and Lord Halsbury's simple words about a real thing have a ring of practical truth. To think of a company as a set of rules is helpful up to a point and does shed some light on the subject of company responsibility. Yet it also seems to miss something. The Common People whom the Hamlyn Lectures are supposed to serve might sense that there is more to many companies than that. The McDonald's Corporation has spent more than 300 days in the High Court in The Strand, in the longest trial in British history, demonstrating its own reality. A kind of anthropomorphism would be very hard to eradicate from this branch of the law. Perhaps it is not over-bold to predict that one day a company will be found guilty of murder and that on another day a company will be credited with performing a life-saving operation.[80]

First Hamlyn Lecture
November 7, 1996
Inner Temple

---

[80] For contemporary detailed and scholarly discussions of the issues, see Professor C. M. V. Clarkson *Kicking Corporate Bodies and Damning Their Souls* (1996) 59 M.L.R. 557 and G. R. Sullivan *The Attribution of Culpability to Limited Companies* [1996] C.L.J. 515.

One Golden Thread?

"Throughout the web of the English Criminal Law one golden thread is always to be seen, that it is the duty of the prosecution to prove the prisoner's guilt subject to what I have already said as to the defence of insanity and subject also to any statutory exception."

Woolmington v. Director of Public Prosecutions [1935] A.C. 462, 581, *per* Viscount Sankey L.C.

A kind of Parkinson's law applies to murder trials arising from shooting by firearms. The incidence of a defence of accident increases in proportion to the strength of the Crown's evidence of identity. Every Judge who sits much in Crime becomes aware of this phenomenon. Self-defence is often run and has the advantage if successful of bringing about complete acquittal, but it is naturally of limited scope. Provocation is usually more realistic, but it has the disadvantages of a partly objective test (the self-control of a reasonable person with the accused's characteristics) and of doing no more than reducing the crime to manslaughter. Insanity requires medical evidence and the onus is on the accused; moreover juries can be reluctant to accept even the strongest medical opinion. The modern statutory defence of diminished responsibility can be a more promising runner, but again carries a defence onus and at best a manslaughter verdict. Duress of circumstances is not available for murder, attempted murder or some forms of treason, and fits only most exceptional facts.[1] Automatism and voluntary drunkenness so complete that the accused literally did not know what he or she was doing are desperate defences, and in England the latter again only reduces murder to

---

[1] *R. v. Pommell* [1995] 2 Cr.App.R.607; *R. v. Gotts* [1992] 2 A.C. 412.

manslaughter.[2] On the whole accident is probably more popular with defence counsel.

Consider now the string of misfortunes which befell the appellant in *Woolmington v. Director of Public Prosecutions*. His evidence was that his young wife had left him and gone back to her mother. To persuade her to return he wished to frighten her into thinking that otherwise he would commit suicide. He sawed off the barrels of a rook gun, and threw away into a brook the sawn-off pieces and the hacksaw. He loaded the gun with the only two available cartridges. He attached some wire flex to the gun so that he could suspend it from his shoulder. Wearing his coat over the gun, he bicycled to the house where she was living. She said she was not coming back, but going into service. So he threatened to shoot himself, and to show her the gun brought it across his waist, when it somehow went off by pure accident. He left the house and rode away. His wife's aunt, who was living next door, testified to hearing him say something to the effect "are you coming home?": there was then the slamming of a door, his voice in the kitchen, his going out and getting on his bicycle: she called out to him, but he only looked at her hard and rode away. She found her niece shot through the heart.

When charged that night with murder the appellant unfortunately did not mention that the shooting was accidental. "I want to say nothing, except I done it … It was jealousy I suppose … " So too, earlier he had separately told his mother and his employer simply that he had shot his wife. Unluckily again, a note was found in his coat pocket. It included "They have ruined me and I'll have my revenge … Her mother is no good on this earth but have no more cartridges only two; one for her and one for me …" He explained in evidence that this was written after his wife's death.

He was tried first at Taunton before (Viscount) Finlay J. and a jury. That Judge summed up on the lines that the onus was on the Crown throughout. After a retirement of only an hour and 25 minutes the jury were allowed to disagree. History does not relate why a disagreement was accepted so soon. The second trial was

---

[2] *Director of Public Prosecutions v. Majewski* [1977] A.C. 443. In other Commonwealth countries extreme intoxication is generally regarded as negativing *mens rea* in all crimes: see Smith and Hogan, Criminal Law, (8th ed. 1996) p. 237; but evidence of that degree of intoxication is very rare. Yet in a high proportion of crimes alcohol does play some part.

before Swift J. and a jury at Bristol. This time the jury brought in a guilty verdict after only an hour and nine minutes. The Judge's summing up may have contributed to the result, for he told them in effect that in the circumstances the accused was guilty unless he could satisfy them that his wife's death was due to an accident. He said:[3]

> "The killing of a human being is homicide, however he may be killed, and all homicide is presumed to be malicious and murder, unless the contrary appears from circumstances of alleviation, excuse, or justification. 'In every charge of murder, the fact of killing being first proved, all the circumstances of accident, necessity, or infirmity are to be satisfactorily proved by the prisoner, unless they arise out of the evidence produced against him; for the law presumeth the fact to have been founded in malice, unless the contrary appeareth.' Foster's *Crown Law* (1762), p.255. That has been the law of this country for all time since we had law. Once it is shown to a jury that somebody has died through the act of another, that is presumed to be murder, unless the person who has been guilty of the act which causes the death can satisfy a jury that what happened was something less, something which might be alleviated, something which might be reduced to a charge of manslaughter, or was something which was accidental, or was something which could be justified."

The appellant's ill-luck continued. The Court of Criminal Appeal (Avory, Lawrence and Graves–Lord JJ., the judgment being given by Avory J.) dismissed his appeal. They said "it may be that it would have been better"[4] if the Judge had told the jury that if they entertained reasonable doubt whether they should accept the accused's explanation they should either acquit him altogether or convict him of manslaughter only; but the Court relied on the statutory proviso allowing the dismissal of an appeal if they [the Court] consider that no substantial miscarriage of justice has actually occurred.[5]

---

[3] [1935] A.C. at 465.
[4] 25 Cr. App. R.72, 75. Lord Sankey rendered the Court of Appeal's "would" as "might"—see [1935] A.C. at 470—which was not an improvement.
[5] The test commonly applied, built on *Woolmington*, is whether a reasonable jury, after being properly directed, would, on the evidence properly admissible without doubt convict: *Stirland v. Director of Public Prosecutions* [1944] A.C. 315, 321, per Viscount Simon L.C. Perhaps this represents a shelving of responsibility by the courts, the more significant in the days when the Court of Criminal Appeal in England had no power to order a new trial. In *Woolmington* itself the House of Lords differed from the Court of Criminal Appeal by declining to apply the proviso. Viscount Sankey gave only brief and general reasons for this, whereas

Thirty five years later, in delivering the judgment of the Privy Council in *Jayasena v. The Queen*,[6] Lord Devlin quoted the phrase that I have quoted as evidence that for some considerable time before 1935 many English Judges had in practice been applying the law with less strictness towards the defence than the terms warranted. A further possibility is that Avory J. wished to avoid expressing an opinion on a difficult point, for he accepted that there was ample old authority for Swift J.'s statement of the law.

The appellant's case was then allowed to go to the House of Lords, where at last his misfortunes ended. Some personalia are not without interest. The Lord Chancellor of the day, Viscount Sankey, presided. A convert politically to the Labour Party after the experience of chairing in 1919 a Commission on the Coal-Mining Industry (he recommended nationalisation), he was appointed Lord Chancellor in 1929 by Ramsay MacDonald. He is described[7] as the author of judgments "clear, careful and correct, but they do not entitle him to a place among the great English judges" although he had "the ability to rise to the heights when necessary". The most senior of the Lords of Appeal who sat with the Lord Chancellor was Lord Hewart, the Lord Chief Justice. No doubt this relatively rare instance of a Lord Chief Justice participating in the judicial work of the House of Lords is to be put down to the nature of the issue, an important one in the administration of the criminal law. The invitation seems less likely to have reflected personal admiration, for a few months previously Hewart in his maiden speech in the House had departed from convention (maiden speeches are supposed to be non-controversial) by launching a violent attack on Sankey.[8] "Almost incoherent with rage" and in "spluttering and menacing words", he complained of a provision in a Bill which authorised the Master of the Rolls to appoint one of the Lords Justices to preside over the second Appeal Court, instead of this being a matter of seniority. Another sidelight is that Rigby Swift, whose summing up was in

---

Avory J.'s analysis of the evidence was fairly devastating. Contrast [1935] A.C. at 482–3 with 25 Cr. App. R. at 76–9. In the result the appellant was acquitted because of what was held to be Swift J.'s mistake.

[6] [1970] A.C. 618. 625.

[7] R.F.V. Heuston, *Lives of the Lord Chancellors 1885–1940*, 525. Apart from *Woolmington*, Heuston refers to Canadian constitutional cases in the Privy Council.

[8] Heuston op.cit. 519–20.

question, had been Hewart's frequent opponent at the Bar when they were leaders of the Northern Circuit.[9]

A less obviously qualified participant in the *Woolmington* hearing was Lord Tomlin, a Chancery Judge especially experienced in patent work; but then there were two common lawyers almost universally regarded as in the first judicial rank, Lord Atkin and Lord Wright. Atkin had a famous gift for a memorable phrase. It is tempting to speculate that the golden thread figure of speech was his. It is more colourful than Sankey's usual style. But I have no solid evidence for this suggestion.

It was a rather misleading figure of speech. A gaze at the web of the English Criminal Law would certainly not have revealed any such golden thread. Since at least 1762 it had been generally understood by lawyers, as indeed Viscount Sankey accepted, that on a murder charge the onus was on the accused, once it was proved that he or she had killed the deceased, to satisfy the jury of defences such as accident. Presumably there were countless summings up to that effect, and consequent executions. It was a harsh rule before the Act of 1898 enabling the prisoner to give evidence. Yet perhaps, at least since that Act, it is not incapable of justification by reason of the very gravity of homicide. So Sir Michael Foster thought in 1762.[10] It was "very right" that "the law presumeth the fact [of murder] to have been founded in malice." And, as Sir John Smith has drawn to attention,[11] after *Woolmington*

---

[9] See the entry for Swift in the Dictionary of National Biography 1931–1940, contributed by John E. Singleton (Singleton L.J.). Opinions of Hewart as a Judge vary a little. In his D.N.B. entry, 1941–1950, H.G. Hanbury mentions that he regarded law as "a mighty engine for the vindication of the fundamental rights of man" and speaks of his courtesy to counsel and his faith in the jury system. But the verdict in D.M. Walker's *Oxford Companion to Law* is that he was "perhaps the worst Chief Justice since the seventeenth century . . . lacking dignity, fairness, and a sense of justice." His most famous dictum was in *R. v. Sussex Justices ex p. McCarthy* [1924] K.B. 256, 259: " . . . it is not merely of some importance but is of fundamental importance that justice should not only be done, but should manifestly and undoubtedly be seen to be done." It is no longer totally reliable: *R. v. Gough* [1993] A.C. 646.

[10] Quoted in [1935] A.C. at 474.

[11] *The Presumption of Innocence* (1987) 38 N.I.L.Q. 223, 225–6. For Lord Goddard's views that the defences of duress and non-insane automatism involved a burden of proof on the defendant, Sir John cites *R. v. Steane* [1947] K.B. 997, rejected in *R. v. Gill* [1963] 1 W.L.R. 841; [1963] 2 All E.R. 688, and *Hill v. Baxter*]1958] 1 Q.B. 277, overruled in *Bratty v. Attorney-General for Northern Ireland* [1963] A.C. 386. He also points out that old authority that the accused bore the onus of proving self-defence prevailed in England until *R. v. Chan Kau* [1955] A.C. 206 and *R. v. Lobell* [1957] 1 Q.B. 547.

a Judge as steeped in the traditions of the common law as Lord Goddard C.J. was not prepared to accept literally the proposition that in trials for common law crimes, subject to statutory exceptions, the onus lies on the Crown to rebut all defences for which there is some evidential foundation, save only insanity. It now appears to be generally accepted, however, not only that this is the modern rule but that it extends to cases of homicide.[12] The closest precedent, indeed the only precedent, which the Lord Chancellor was able to cite for the decision in *Woolmington* was the decision of the Court of Criminal Appeal in *Davies*,[13] when it was held to be a misdirection to tell the jury that it was for the prisoner to satisfy the jury that his gun had gone off accidentally. That was not a murder charge, to which Foster's observations were directed, but a charge of shooting with intent to resist lawful apprehension.

So, in relation to murder at least, *Woolmington* made a great change in the law, a change that has had an incalculable flow-on effect. Sir John Smith hails the decision. "Never, in my opinion, has the House of Lords done a more noble deed in the field of criminal law than on that day."[14] It would be temerarious now to criticise *Woolmington* so far as it applies to grave crime. One must bear in mind also that the International Covenant on Civil and Political Rights, Article 14(2), declares that everyone charged with a criminal offence shall have the right to be presumed innocent until proved guilty according to law, and national Bills of Rights commonly have the same provision.[15] Yet the qualification "according to law" does allow some flexibility as regards the onus of proof when a particular defence is raised.[16] And I must now own to misgivings about some of the consequences of *Woolmington*. To introduce this part of the discussion it should be pointed out that on one potentially important subject, not mentioned in Viscount Sankey's speech, *Woolmington* evidently does not or may not prevail.

---

[12] See for instance Archbold 1996, vol.2, chapter 17 passim.

[13] (1913) 8 Cr. App. R. 211.

[14] 38 N.I.L.Q. at 224.

[15] *e.g.* Canadian Charter of Rights and Freedoms, s.11(d);
New Zealand Bill of Rights Act 1990, s.25(c). So, too, the European Convention on Human Rights, Article 6(2)

[16] *Attorney-General of Hong Kong v. Lee Kwong-kut* [1993] A.C. 951.

BIGAMY

Bigamy is rarely prosecuted today, a fact doubtless partly attributable to the increasing popularity and even acceptability of *de facto* unions, but the law relating to it is important in principle. It is a statutory crime, created by the Offences against the Person Act 1861, s.57, committed according to the words of the section by any person who, being married, marries any other person during the life of the former husband or wife. The statutory description "former" seems illogical in a country where monogamy prevails (as is the position in the United Kingdom) but it has apparently never been successfully argued that it is a good defence that the lawful marriage is still subsisting. A proviso to the section does afford, however, certain defences. In particular nothing in the section shall extend to any person marrying a second time whose husband or wife shall have been continually absent from such person for the space of seven years last past, and shall not have been known by such person to be living within that time.

In *R. v. Tolson*[17] the accused had gone through a ceremony of marriage within seven years after she had been deserted by her husband. So she did not come within the proviso. But the jury found that at the time of the second ceremony she in good faith and on reasonable grounds believed her husband to be dead. On a case reserved, no less than 14 Judges sat—which would be regarded today as a highly extravagant use of judicial resources. By a majority of nine to five it was held that the jury's finding established a defence to the indictment. The importance of the decision lies in its application to the statutory offence of what was accepted to be the common law principle that "an honest and reasonable belief in circumstances, which, if true, would make the act for which the prisoner is indicted an innocent act has always been treated to be a good defence."[18] The judgments contain no suggestion that the onus of proof as to this defence falls otherwise than on the defendant. Their unmistakable tenor is that it is for the defendant to establish the defence affirmatively.

In *R. v. Wheat*[19] the jury found that at the time of the alleged bigamous marriage the prisoner believed in good faith on reasonable grounds that he had been divorced. The Court of Criminal

---

[17] (1889) 23 Q.B.D. 168
[18] *Per* Cave J. at 181
[19] [1921] 2 K.B. 119.

Appeal, in a judgment of five judges delivered by Avory J., held that belief in divorce was materially different from belief in a spouse's death, and that Cave J. in *Tolson* had stated the law too widely. They also held that there was no evidence on which the jury could find belief on reasonable grounds. For both reasons the prisoner stood convicted.

In *R. v. Carswell*[20] the jury made the same finding as the jury had made in *R v. Wheat*. A Court of Appeal of nine Judges was convened, a very rare occurrence in New Zealand. It was a close run thing, but by a majority of five to four the Court declined to follow *Wheat* and applied the wider *Tolson* principle. The majority did contrive to discern some difference in the statutory language, but a reading of their judgment brings out clearly enough that it was impelled by the simple proposition that "it is not a wrong act for a man who believes he has obtained a divorce to get married again."[21] That was followed by a reference to *reasonable* belief.

Carswell was a courageous decision in its day, for in that era there was much more heel-clicking deference to English authority. The next stage in the story is that in 1937 a similar question divided the High Court of Australia. On this occasion there was the immaterial refinement that the accused was found by the jury to have reasonably believed at the time of the "former" marriage that it was invalid because he understood that the wife's decree nisi of divorce had not been made absolute. By a majority of three to two the same result was reached as had been reached in New Zealand in *Carswell* and for essentially the same reasons. Of the various judgments, however, only that of Dixon J. made any reference to *Carswell* and even he incorrectly described it[22] as a decision of the Supreme Court of New Zealand (equivalent then to the English High Court or the Supreme Courts of the Australian States).

In *R. v. Gould*[23] the matter was reconsidered in England. The question was whether it was a good defence that the defendant at the time of the "second" marriage honestly and reasonably held the mistaken belief that a decree absolute dissolving his previous marriage had been granted. The Court of Appeal now repudiated *Wheat*. In delivering the judgment Diplock L.J. made much of the

---

[20] [1926] N.Z.L.R. 321.
[21] [1926] N.Z.L.R. at 339, per Sim J.
[22] 59 C.L.R. at 308.
[23] [1968] 2 Q.B. 65. There was an intervening English case of *R. v. King* [1964] 1 Q.B. 285 not calling for further notice in the present context.

Australian case of *Thomas*, being especially laudatory of Sir Owen Dixon, but did not mention the more pioneering New Zealand case of *Carswell*, doubtless because it had not been cited in argument. It is to be noted that although *Gould* was post-*Woolmington*, Diplock L.J. said nothing about that case. Nor had the Australian Court done so in *Thomas*. At this point in the history one can scarcely doubt that, as Dixon J. put it in the course of his elaborate judgment,[24] it was open to the accused in answer to the bigamy charge to exculpate himself by *showing* that on reasonable grounds he mistakenly believed in facts which, if true, would make his earlier marriage void; and that this was an instance, as Dixon J. also put it, of the "reasonable doctrine that when a statute introduced into our criminal law a new offence it should be understood prima facie to intend the offence to take its place in a coherent general system and to be governed by the established principles of criminal responsibility."[25] Nor was there any ground for thinking that the common law of England, Australia or New Zealand differed on this matter. A prima facie case of bigamy being proved, the onus of proving honest and reasonable mistake was on the defendant, this being an application of a general common law principle regarding mistake.

A GENERAL PRINCIPLE AND ITS EROSION

While it was not easy to reconcile all the cases[26] and Judges may be said to have had a choice of interpretations, it was once widely accepted that prima facie the general principle was applicable to statutory offences. Thus in *Sherras v. De Rutzen*[27] a publican who served liquor to a police constable at a time when the latter was not wearing his armlet was held to have a good defence to a charge of supplying a constable on duty. Day J. said that the only inference that he drew from the omission of the word "knowingly" in the relevant subsection was that the defendant had to prove that he did not know: it would be straining the law to say that a publican acting in the bona fide belief that the constable was off duty, and having reasonable grounds for that belief, was nevertheless guilty of an offence. And that approach was followed in Australia and

[24] 59 C.L.R. at 309.
[25] *Ibid.* 304.
[26] *Sherras v. De Rutzen* [1895] 1 Q.B. 918, 921, per R. S. Wright J.
[27] Cit. *supra*.

New Zealand. In the broadly similar case of *Maher v. Musson*,[28] pre-*Woolmington*, Dixon J. himself pronounced, in an echo of Cave J. in *Tolson*,—

> "... in the case alike of an offence at common law and, unless expressly or impliedly excluded by the enactment, of a statutory offence, it is a good defence that the accused held an honest and reasonable belief in the existence of circumstances, which, if true, would make innocent the act for which he is charged."

Dixon J. went on to say that the absolute language of the statute there in question should be treated as doing no more than throwing upon the defendant chemist the burden of exculpating himself by showing that he reasonably thought the spirits which he had bought were not illicit.[29] In fact they had been stolen, but he claimed unsuccessfully not to have suspected this. It was a variant of the kind of case so common in criminal courts of purchase of hot property from an unknown stranger in a public house or coming upon it after it has fallen from a lorry.

I will turn to the New Zealand struggle shortly. But first it has to be said that Sir Owen Dixon, seldom one to stray far from what he perceived to be the orthodox path, became hesitant and cryptic. There is a suspicion that he did so under the influence of *Woolmington*, although if so he did not disclose it. The case was in 1941, *Proudman v. Dayman*,[30] when Dixon J. joined in a decision that, on a charge of permitting an unlicensed person to drive a motor vehicle on a road, proof that the defendant knew that the driver was unlicensed was unnecessary. In a studiously non-committal judgment he distinguished between statutes whose purpose is "to add a new crime to the general criminal law" and those where "in matters of police, of health, of safety or the like the legislature adopts penal provisions in order to cast on the individual the responsibility of so ordering his affairs that the general welfare will not be prejudiced." The general rule about the availability of honest and reasonable mistake as a defence he still saw as possibly applying prima facie to summary offences created by modern statutes, but the presumption was only a weak one and the marked and growing tendency was to treat the prima facie rule as excluded. If it was not excluded, the defendant bore the burden in

[28] (1934) 52 C.L.R. 100, 104.
[29] *Ibid*. 105.
[30] 67 C.L.R. 536.

the first place. "The burden may not finally rest upon him of satisfying the tribunal in case of doubt."[31] Justly, Smith and Hogan describe these observations as equivocal.[32]

The same authors say,[33] and likewise justly, that in the case where ambiguity set in at the highest judicial level in England also, "The five speeches ... differ so greatly, and it is so difficult to make sense of parts of them that courts in later cases have found it impossible to extract a *ratio decidendi*." They regard it as "another calamitous decision by the House". This is *Warner v. Metropolitan Police Commissioner*.[34] A majority (Lord Reid dissenting) held that a statutory offence of possessing certain scheduled drugs was absolute: whether the accused possessed them with an innocent or a guilty mind was immaterial. A number of opinions were expressed on what amounts to possession. Only Lord Pearce referred to *Woolmington*, saying that unfortunately he did not find a half-way house reconcilable with Viscount Sankey's speech, but that it would be an improvement if Parliament were to enact that when a person has ownership or physical possession of drugs he should be guilty unless he proves on a balance of probabilities that he was unaware of their nature or had reasonable excuse for their possession.[35] Parliament did soon pass ameliorating legislation on these lines,[36] so providing evidence that a defence of proved total absence of fault—a phrase to which I will return—is acceptable even in the serious criminal field of hard drugs.

Whereas Lord Reid had been the only champion of *mens rea* in the speeches in *Warner*, his approach was shared all five Law Lords who sat 18 months later in *Sweet v. Parsley*.[37] On a charge against the occupier of permitting premises to be used for the smoking of cannabis resin, their Lordships held unanimously that it was the purposes of the occupier (not temporary users) to which the section referred: there must be knowledge or acquiescence on her part: the court ought not to class an offence as absolute unless that must have been the intention of Parliament. After speaking of the extremes of full *mens rea* (difficult to prove) on the one hand and

---

[31] *Ibid*. 541.
[32] 8th ed. 122.
[33] *Ibid*. 113.
[34] [1969] 2 A.C. 256.
[35] *Ibid*. 303 and 307.
[36] Misuse of Drugs Act 1971, s.28. For details of the legislation and the case law on it, see 11(1) Halsbury's Laws of England, (4th ed. 1990) Reissue para. 404.
[37] [1970] A.C. 132.

absolute offences (leading to some manifestly unjust convictions and bringing the administration of justice into public scandal) on the other, Lord Reid said that Parliament had not infrequently transferred the onus as regards *mens rea* to the accused, so that, once the necessary facts were proved, he had to convince the jury that on the balance of probabilities he was innocent of any criminal intention. "I find it a little surprising that more use has not been made of this method; but one of the bad effects of the decision of this House in *Woolmington* ... may have been to discourage its use."[38] There followed in Lord Reid's speech favourable mention of what Cave J. had said in *Tolson* and of part of what Dixon J. had said in *Proudman*. Lord Pearce similarly spoke[39] of the half-way house as attractive, while alluding to the obstacle created by *Woolmington*. He noted that the half-way house had not been argued for. Lord Diplock[40] cited *Maher, Thomas, Tolson, Gould,* and *Wheat*; only to stop short of hinting that his own judgment in *Gould* had not treated *Woolmington* as relevant and would give the impression that the onus as to the defence of honest and reasonable mistake fell on the defendant. He continued:

> "*Woolmington's* case affirmed the principle that the onus lies upon the prosecution in a criminal trial to prove all the elements of the offence with which the accused is charged. It does not purport to lay down how that onus can be discharged as respects any particular elements of the offence. This, under our system of criminal procedure, is left to the common sense of the jury. *Woolmington's* case did not decide anything so irrational as that the prosecution must call evidence to prove the absence of any mistaken belief by the accused in the existence of facts which, if true, would make the act innocent, any more than it decided that the prosecution must call evidence to prove the absence of any claim of right in a charge of larceny. The jury is entitled to presume that the accused acted with knowledge of the facts, unless there is some evidence to the contrary originating from the accused who alone can know on what belief he acted and on what ground the belief, if mistaken, was held. What *Woolmington's* case did decide is that where there is any such evidence the jury after considering it and also any relevant evidence called by the prosecution on the issue of the existence of the alleged mistaken belief should acquit the accused unless they feel sure that he did not hold the belief or that there were no reasonable grounds upon which he could have done so.

[38] *Ibid.* 150.
[39] *Ibid.* 157–8.
[40] *Ibid.* 164.

This, as I understand it, is the approach of Dixon J. to the onus of proof of honest and reasonable mistaken belief as he expressed it in *Proudman v. Dayman* (1941) 67 C.L.R. 536, 541. Unlike the position where a statute expressly places the onus of proving lack of guilty knowledge on the accused, the accused does not have to prove the existence of mistaken belief on the balance of probabilities; he has to raise a reasonable doubt as to its non-existence."

As we have seen, Dixon J. did not in truth commit himself to that approach in *Proudman*: rather he drew back guardedly from his pre-*Woolmington* commitment apparent in *Maher*.

At best, then, *Sweet v. Parsley* left the prospect of a half-way house solution in England hazy. Later authorities have not improved the prospect. They have concentrated rather on the stark alternatives of full mens rea and absolute liability as to at least some elements of the offence.[41] The golden thread has not prevented some severe instances of liability being held absolute. For example in England it is apparently an offence, punishable up to a maximum of six months' imprisonment, to drive a motor vehicle on a road while disqualified, even if one neither knows nor ought to know of the disqualification.[42] A reader of the textbooks will not take long to learn that which way the court will go is something of a lottery. A range of considerations has emerged, prominent among which are whether absolute (or "strict") liability will be more effective to achieve the objects of the statute, as by promoting greater vigilance in matters of social concern, including public safety;[43] and the ease or difficulty for the respective parties of discharging the burden of proof.[44] But such considerations clash, as in *Pharmaceutical Society of Great Britain v. Storkwain Ltd*[45] where

---

[41] See, for this refinement, *Gammon Ltd v. Attorney-General of Hong Kong* [1985] A.C. 1, 17, *per* Lord Scarman delivering the judgment of the Privy Council.

[42] *Taylor v. Kenyon* [1952] 2 All E.R. 726; *R v. Miller* [1975] 1 W.L.R. 1222; [1975] 2 All E.R. 974; *R. v. Bowsher* [1973] R.T.R. 202; [1973] Crim. L.R. 373; Archbold, 1996 Reissue, vol.2, paras 32–83 and 17–166.

[43] *Gammon*, *cit.supra*.

[44] *R. v. Hunt* [1987] A.C. 352.

[45] [1986] 1 W.L.R. 903; [1986] 2 All E.R. 635. Smith and Hogan, strong supporters of *mens rea*, do not like this decision: see Sir John Smith's eighth edition at 101 and 110. Insofar as the decision imposed on the seller absolute liability for acting on a forged prescription, the opinion of Smith and Hogan appears to have much force. The decision was based on the ground that the Act or Orders under it required a form of *mens rea* for certain other offences, or provided for defences if the defendant could prove that he had exercised due diligence and that the contravention was due to the act or default of another. But none of those provisions seems to have been intended to cover the case of forgery by a person

it was held that a retail pharmacist was guilty of selling a pre-scription-only medicine even if the prescription presented to him was forged and there was nothing more that he could reasonably have done to check its authenticity. Moreover the greater vigilance consideration is open-ended. Deterrence is a principal goal of all criminal liability; and usually the more severe the law, the greater the deterrence. As regards very many offences it will not be diffi-cult for a court to say that absolute liability will be more effective to achieve the objects of the statute.

TOTAL ABSENCE OF FAULT

I must now reveal that New Zealand law has been developing in a different direction. Largely because this is not known in England, I must run over the history.

It began in 1905 with *R. v. Ewart*[46] when the Court of Appeal held by a majority of three to two that it was a defence to a charge of the statutory crime of selling a newspaper containing matter of an indecent, immoral and obscene nature (some evidence in a divorce case had been published) that the defendant did not know that the contents were of that nature. Three classes of case were identified: in short, (i) full *mens rea*; (ii) absolute offence; (iii) cases where the defendant may discharge himself by proving to the satisfaction of the tribunal which tries him that he did not have a guilty mind. The English authorities as they stood at that time were fully—and, I think, fairly—reviewed and, as the majority of the Court thought, followed. *Ewart* was understood to govern this tract of the law of New Zealand for some 65 years. Then in *R. v. Strawbridge*[47] in dealing with a charge of cultivating cannabis the Court of Appeal was faced with (*inter alia*) *Woolmington, Sweet v. Parsley,* and some of the other cases that I have mentioned. In the result the Court said that it was clear that *Ewart* had gone too far in holding that in the third class of case the burden passed to the accused. It was still true, however, that the onus lay on the accused to point to some evidence creating a reasonable doubt that "he did

unknown, which the drafter evidently did not have in mind. On the other hand, in the generality of their argument, and in seeking to place the burden of proof on the prosecution, counsel for the seller may have gone too far. The House of Lords were apparently not asked to consider the question of a defence of total absence of fault as developed in Canada and New Zealand.
[46] 25 N.Z.L.R. 709.
[47] [1970] N.Z.L.R. 909.

not have a guilty mind." Finding the insertion of *sic* in brackets distastefully patronising, I omit it. The meaning of North P. is clear enough.

Sir Alfred North was a strong and much admired Judge. Possibly no admiration for him exceeds my own, as I suspect that he well knew, despite our occasional tussles when at the Bar I argued cases before his court. Nor was he always unduly disposed to follow English authority.[48] In this instance, though, he may have been over-influenced by Lord Diplock.

At all events the New Zealand Courts have since moved away from *Strawbridge* on onus, reverting rather to the English approach before *Woolmington* and to a position corresponding to that which Diplock L.J. had appeared to adopt in *Gould*. Whether or not the movement has any attraction beyond New Zealand, it has been a considered one, accompanied by no little discussion of authorities in other jurisdictions, and I can outline it only briefly in a lecture.

The first seed was perhaps sown in *Police v. Creedon*.[49] One of the Court of Appeal Judges confessed that the more one looked at the reported cases and academic writings, the more confused the picture became; and he indicated that, on a charge against a motorist of failing to yield a right of way, he would have favoured a defence of honest and reasonable mistake, with the burden of proof on the defendant. By 1980 there had become available the notable decision of a court of nine Judges in the Supreme Court of Canada,[50] delivered by Dickson J., that to the "public welfare" offence of causing or permitting the pollution of a creek it was a defence to prove that the defendant took all reasonable care. In *Ministry of Transport v. Burnetts Motors Ltd*,[51] a case of spillage of

---

[48] He was a member of the Judicial Committee of the Privy Council who, in *Australian Consolidated Press Ltd v. Uren* [1969] 1 A.C. 590, declined for Australia to impose the restriction on the categories of cases in which exemplary damages can be awarded which had been introduced in England by the House of Lords in *Rookes v. Barnard* [1964] A.C. 1129. He gave the principal judgment in *Corbett v. Social Security Commission* [1962] N.Z.L.R. 878 to the effect that, notwithstanding the decision of the House of Lords in *Duncan v. Cammell Laird & Co. Ltd* [1942] A.C. 624, the New Zealand Court could overrule a Ministerial objection to the production of documents for which public interest immunity was claimed. He presided over the Court of Appeal which, in *Bognuda v. Upton & Shearer Ltd* [1972] N.Z.L.R. 741, declined to follow *Dalton v. Angus* (1881) 6 App.Cas. 740 and held that a defendant excavating on his own property owed a duty of care for the protection of his neighbour's wall.

[49] [1976] 1 N.Z.L.R. 571, 584 *et seq.*

[50] *R. v. City of Sault Ste Marie* [1978] 85 D.L.R. (3^d) 161.

[51] [1980] 1 N.Z.L.R. 51.

offensive matter on a highway, it was accordingly suggested that the same solution might be appropriate in New Zealand, although on the evidence there the defence could not succeed.

Then in *Civil Aviation Department v. MacKenzie*[52] the break-through came, a majority in the Court of Appeal of three Judges to one holding that, to a charge of the regulatory offence of opera-ting an aircraft in a manner causing unnecessary danger to persons or property, total absence of fault was a defence. The defendant aviator had not seen some telephone wires which he struck. Next, in *Hastings City Council v. Simmons*,[53] the Court of Appeal gave a local authority prosecuted for discharging waste (through a rubbish tip) into natural water an opportunity of establishing total absence of fault.

Quite a gruelling effort at scrutinising the overall position as to *mens rea* in statutory offences was undertaken in *Millar v. Ministry of Transport*.[54] The charge was driving while disqualified. Unani-mously a court of five applied the ordinary presumption that mens rea was an ingredient: to raise the issue the defendant would have to point, however, to some evidence that he did not know of the disqualification. *Taylor v. Kenyon* and the other English cases treating this as an absolute offence were not followed. It was noted that in the decade since *Creedon* authorities in the various jurisdictions had become, if anything, even more confusing. The Court identified at least seven categories into which a statutory offences might be held to fall. In a struggle for simplicity, however, it was suggested that the three basic alternatives are (i) full *mens rea*; (ii) absolute or "strict" liability; (iii) a defence of total absence of fault.

This approach seems to have proved reasonably workable and not to have caused injustice. I list a few High Court decisions applying it. In *Ministry of Transport v. Crawford*[55] a defence of total absence of fault was held to be available, not indeed to a motorist who had taken alcoholic drink not realising that it was of abnormal strength, but to a motorist who had taken drink which he reason-

[52] [1983] N.Z.L.R. 78.

[53] [1984] 2 N.Z.L.R. 502.

[54] [1986] 1 N.Z.L.R. 660. See also *Waaka v. Police* [1987] 1 N.Z.L.R. 754 as to what the prosecution must prove to make out a charge of assaulting a police constable in the execution of his duty. Full *mens rea* was held to be required. I add the Australian authority of the *He Kaw Teh v. R.* (1985) 157 C.L.R. 523, a case relating to prohibited imports, which goes on essentially similar lines.

[55] [1988] 1 N.Z.L.R. 762, Tipping J.

Learning Resources Centre

ably thought contained no alcohol. In *Re Wairarapa Election Petition*[56] the defence was held to be available to a parliamentary candidate charged with the corrupt practice of paying more than $5000 for election expenses; but it was found that the defence was not established on the facts. In *Police v. Starkey*[57] it was held that the defence was available to a charge of publishing untrue statements defamatory of a rival local authority election candidate: the defendant had to show on the balance of probabilities that reasonable care had been taken to ensure the truth of the statements.

In *Keech v. Pratt*[58] a defendant, having sensibly decided not to ride his motor cycle after drinking at a nightclub, had the misfortune to be assaulted and suffer concussion while he was walking home. He then rode the motor cycle and was apprehended by a constable. He was over the limit, but the defence was held to be sustainable if he could prove that he was acting as an automaton. This decision, although obviously debatable as to onus, perhaps suggests a more realistic approach to alleged automatism than that hitherto conventional. As has been mentioned,[59] Lord Goddard favoured the same approach whenever automatism was raised as a criminal defence.

Last I note a recent decision[60] concerning a charge against an employer of failing to take all reasonably practicable steps to ensure the safety of its employees. The employer had provided clothing protecting, as far as reasonably practicable, against the hazard of direct harm from a furnace explosion. The question was whether better protection should have been provided against the risk of the overalls themselves igniting. Alternative uniforms with various advantages and disadvantages were available. It was found that, in balancing the risk and making the selection, the defendant had acted as a diligent and reasonably responsible employer. Absence of fault was established and the defendant acquitted. The case required and received a thorough investigation of the facts, after full disclosure by the employer. It appears to be an admirable example of the defence of total absence of fault in practice.

[56] [1988] 2 N.Z.L.R. 74, Full Court of High Court, Davison C.J., Greig and Wylie JJ.
[57] [1989] 2 N.Z.L.R. 373, Barker J.
[58] [1994] 1 N.Z.L.R. 65, Greig J.
[59] *Supra*, n.11.
[60] *Buchanans Foundry Ltd v. Department of Labour* [1996] 3 N.Z.L.R. 112, Hansen J.

ADVANTAGES OF A VIA MEDIA

I must remove two possible misconceptions. First, it should not be thought that the New Zealand Courts are shying away from the ordinary *Woolmington* rule that the onus is on the prosecution of proving guilt. Indeed, in *Millar* itself the presumption that *mens rea* has to be proved was held not to be displaced. Rejecting, as we have seen, the English solution of absolute liability, the Court of Appeal held that to sheet home a charge of driving while disqualified the prosecutor had to prove beyond reasonable doubt that the defendant knew of the disqualification or was wilfully blind to it. When, however, a disqualification order had been pronounced in the usual way in open court, the *evidential* onus would fall on the defendant of pointing to something in the evidence raising doubt about his knowledge. In fact in *Millar* there was room for confusion as to the term of the relevant disqualification, a District Court Judge having made orders on a number of charges at the same sitting. The proceedings had dragged on, and the Court of Appeal decided in all the circumstances that justice required an acquittal.

The Canadian case law is instructive. The Canadian Charter of Rights and Freedoms guarantees fundamental justice (section 7) and the presumption of innocence (section 11(d)) but these rights are subject to such reasonable limits prescribed by law as can be demonstrably justified in a free and democratic society (section 1). As to grave crimes, the Supreme Court has declined to allow the presumption of innocence to be overridden in any respect. For murder, an accused must be proved beyond reasonable doubt to have intended or foreseen the likelihood of death; it is not enough, for instance, that he has caused the death in the course of a burglary.[61] The statutory offence of selling or buying stolen rock containing precious metals has also been seen as a truly criminal offence involving activity bereft of social utility and repugnant in the eyes of society. A reverse onus clause casting on the accused the burden of proving that he was the owner or the agent of the owner is accordingly unconstitutional; but is to be read down (that is to say, in effect amended by the Court) to cast on the accused merely an evidential onus of raising a reasonable doubt on the matter.[62]

By contrast, reverse onus in public welfare offences[63] has sur-

---

[61] *R. v. Martineau* [1990] 2 S.C.R. 633; *R. v. Sit* (1991) 8 C.R.R. (2d) 317.

[62] *R. v. Laba* (1944) 120 D.L.R. (4th) 175.

[63] See the *City of Sault Ste Marie* case, n.50 *supra*.

vived the Charter. *R. v. Wholesale Travel Group Inc.*[64] was concerned with a charge of false or misleading advertising contrary to a Competition Act. A maximum of five years imprisonment could be imposed. By a majority decision of the Supreme Court, a reverse onus clause was held constitutional to the extent that it required the accused to prove error and due diligence. Further requirements of the statutory defence as to corrective advertising were, however, held unconstitutional. The latter refinement aside, the interesting feature of the decision is the distinction drawn between truly criminal conduct and conduct prohibited in the public interest by the regulation of certain activities ("regulatory offences"). As Cory J. said,[65] "It is absolutely essential that governments have the ability to enforce a standard of reasonable care in activities affecting public welfare . . . the standard of reasonable care has been accepted by the regulated actor upon entering the regulated sphere."

Like many lines, the line between true crimes and regulatory offences will not always be easy to draw. Still, we can sense a solid distinction. And in the second category, if to impose the full burden of proving *mens rea* on the prosecution would tend to frustrate the purpose of the statute, the developments in Canada and New Zealand which I have attempted to explain offer the possibility of a via media short of absolute liability. It should not be thought, either, that the defence of total absence of fault represents a soft option. The word "total", perhaps unnecessary, has been used for emphasis. Although no case has yet sharply raised the point, a defendant company invoking the defence will have to prove, for instance, that on the balance of probabilities all its employees taking part in the relevant operation exercised reasonable care. Thus, while the *Storkwain* defendant would almost certainly have had a good defence, and conceivably also the defendant in *Warner*, it seems less likely that the defence would have been made out in the building plans deviation case of *Gammon* (the facts had not been fully determined at the stage of the Privy Council appeal) or in the sex establishment licensing case of *Westminster City Council v. Croyalgrange Ltd.*[66] The defendant company in the river pollution

---

[64] 84 D.L.R. (4th) 161.

[65] *Ibid.* 220–1.

[66] [1986] 1 W.L.R. 674; [1986] 2 All E.R. 353. Similarly the defendant might not have been able to establish all reasonable care in the crocidolite case of *Atkinson v. Sir Alfred McAlpine & Son Ltd* (1974) 16 K.I.R. 695; [1974] Cr.L.R. 668, discussed in *Smith and Hogan*, 8th ed. 115–6.

case of *Alphacell Ltd v. Woodward*[67] might have had a prospect of establishing the defence: compare that case with *Hastings City Council v. Simmons* and *Sault Ste Marie*.

Sir John Smith ended his 1987 MacDermott Lecture on *The Presumption of Innocence*[68] with the indisputable proposition that in England the golden thread has always been broken at some points, adding "It would be a great day for our law if the golden thread could be made to run truly throughout the tangled web." I am, with full respect, not so sure. But it does seem odd that in the home of *Woolmington* absolute (or "strict") liability is so extensively accepted by the courts, and with some equanimity. It is as if the great case has created a judicial mindset which recoils at a shifting of the onus, yet tolerates a harsher solution. The New Zealand via media cannot be claimed to solve all the problems and awaits further working out. Perhaps, though, it would at least be worth looking at in England.

Ultimately the issue is one of relative values. In the eyes of common lawyers and probably in the eyes of the Common People of the Hamlyn Trust, absolute liability for alleged criminal conduct goes against the grain. Nevertheless, for lesser offences, the English courts accept it from time to time, usually in the name of legislative intent—even although in truth the legislature may have been content to leave a practical solution to the courts. A practical solution must allow for the dictates of public expediency in the matter of regulatory offences. The creation of such offences may be the most efficient method of controlling conduct in an industry, but because of the limitations of the prosecution's knowledge the difficulty of proof may be excessively demanding. Then the public interest may well be sufficiently served by casting a burden of proof, or the balance of probabilities, on the defendant. Justice is not denied to the individual if, in the typical case where the defence of total absence of fault can be allowed, it is recognised that he enters a field of activity having a public impact, knowing that in cases of doubt it will be for him to prove that he runs a tight ship.

Second Hamlyn Lecture
November 14, 1996
De Montford University

---

[67] [1972] A.C. 824.
[68] 38 N.I.L.Q. 223.

The Temptation of Elegance Resisted

"Mr Gardiner ... has not been able to cite a single case in which a defendant has been held liable for a careless statement leading, otherwise than through the channel of physical damage, to financial loss."

Hedley Byrne & Co. Ltd v. Heller & Partners Ltd [1964] A.C. 465, 515, *per* Lord Devlin.

This is the third lecture in a series of four arranged to be delivered in different venues. The audiences are therefore different, and it is safe to say that few, if any, persons will hear more than one of the lectures, nor assuredly will any suffer more than two, apart from the lecturer himself and (I believe) one exceptionally resolute scholar. There are other differences. This evening's audience is essentially learned. That alone may not be enough to distinguish it from the audiences in the Inner Temple, De Montfort and Oxford, as they would quickly point out, but there is the added factor that this is something of a homecoming. According to Garter King of Arms, I am of Cambridge in the County of Cambridgeshire. To mark this privilege I propose to treat the audience with a degree of familiarity by taking the liberty of asking it questions—although only mental answers are expected. I would ask you to answer mutely who are the respective authors of the following quotations, each of which has a bearing on the content of the lecture.

1. " ... the temptation of elegance ... can attract us all, simply because a solution, if elegant, automatically carries a degree of credibility; and yet the law has to reflect life in all its untidy complexity ... "

2. "Change need not be, and often is not, as devastating as the fall of Constantinople."

3. "If I were asked what is the most potent influence upon a court in formulating a statement of legal principle, I would answer that in the generality of instances it is the desired result in the particular case before the court."

4. " ... a judge is entitled to take into account that simple fairness ought to be the basis of every legal rule."

5. "There was a fine cellar. When Lord Goddard, an exacting guest, came to dinner he exclaimed 'What is this?' with totally unconcealed astonishment after the first sip of the first wine."

6. " ... an opinion [of a Judge] should not invoke public policy unless it can cite a source for it."

7. *"By definition an increment is bound to take matters further than they are already."*

8. "The basing of the decision on the notion of assumption of responsibility may ... prove the Achilles heel of the majority judgments."

9. "The subject of compensation for personal injuries and death is ... too important ... to be left to the courts. Sooner or later Parliament, instead of tinkering with the tort system, as in the recent limited reforms relating to damages and the procedural changes proposed by the Woolf Report, will have to return to the question of community responsibility for the disabled, including victims of accidents."

10. "The limitations on the doctrine of consideration led to the elaborate yet ultimately unsatisfactory doctrine of assumption of responsibility in *Hedley Byrne*. The way to create liability in situations 'equivalent to contract' was surely to broaden the conception of contract."

11. " ... the present case is not clearly covered by authority. When such a situation is encountered in the field of negligence law, it seems to me that the proper approach, as indicated by all the leading modern authorities from *Donoghue v. Stevenson*[1] onwards, is to look at all the material facts in combination, in order to decide as a question of mixed law and fact whether or not liability should be imposed. Ultimately it may be simply what Lord Morris of Borth-y-Gest was content to call a decision as to whether it is fair and reasonable that a duty of care should arise *(Dorset Yacht Co. Ltd v. Home Office*[2]); or it may be described as a question of the policy of the common law, which is the way in which Lord Denning and Sachs LJ looked on

[1] [1932] A.C. 562.
[2] [1970] A.C. 1004, 1039.

the *Bognor Regis* case.[3] Lord Pearson said in the *Dorset Yacht* case that to some extent the decision in that case must be 'a matter of impression and instinctive judgment as to what is fair and just'.[4] That applies equally to the present case. But it is more than Chancellor's-foot justice. The courts have evolved signposts or guidelines or relevant considerations—involving such notions as neighbours, control, foresight, proximity, opportunity for intermediate examination, deeds or words, the degree and kind of risk to be guarded against—and these are all available to be used as aids to the end result."

Do not be dismayed if you have recognised only one or two, or even none. It would be only an extremely odd person who recognised them all, as he or she would happen to have been reading exactly the same materials as I have recently. Let it be added that two, namely the second (about change) and the seventh (about increment), have been included simply to illustrate how blindingly obvious some of the apparently momentous propositions of learned, and even beguiling, Judges and scholars can be. I will not specify those two writers beyond saying that other, less evident, propositions of theirs are in the list also. The first and third quotations (about elegance and the desired result) are taken from Robert Goff's Maccabaean Lecture in Jurisprudence, 1983, *The Search for Principle*.[5] The fourth (about fairness) would in New Zealand arouse instantly the suspicion that I had said it; but in fact it is from the respectable source of Lord Steyn's Sultan Azlan Shah Lecture, *Contract Law: Fulfilling the Reasonable Expectations of Honest Men*, delivered in Kuala Lumpur last month.

The fifth (wine) is from Robert Heuston's 1993 study of Lord Devlin (Heuston's last prosopography?) to be found in the *Proceedings of the British Academy*, vol.84, 247. Its relevance is that the speech of Lord Devlin in *Hedley Byrne*[6] has probably emerged as the most influential in that highly influential case,[7] and I am going to suggest that it is indeed a vintage speech. On that point I will venture to disagree with the opinions separately expressed in two of the other quotations. The sixth (insisting that Judges depart from their proper sphere if they create public policy) comes from

[3] [1972] 1 Q.B. 373, 390, 400.
[4] [1970] A.C. 1004, 1054.
[5] Proceedings of British Academy, vol.69, 169.
[6] *Hedley Byrne & Co. Ltd v. Heller & Partners Ltd* [1964] A.C. 465.
[7] See for instance *Henderson v. Merrett Syndicates Ltd* [1995] 2 A.C. 145, 178–81, *per* Lord Goff of Chieveley.

a Monsanto Lecture, published as this audience will expect in the Valparaiso University Law Review,[8] by Hans A. Linde, a former Judge of the Oregon Supreme Court. The eighth is one of the fruits of the experience of Professor Basil Markesinis in the House of Lords in *White v. Jones*.[9]

The ninth and tenth (community responsibility and enlarging contract) are from a courageous and stimulating lecture, *Negligence: The Search for Coherence*, delivered in London in recent weeks, in the *Current Legal Problems Series*, by Professor Bob Hepple.

The eleventh, the longer one, I must admit that I did write[10]— 21 years ago, as a young Judge wrestling with the issue whether a purchaser of a truck could recover damages from a Government Department whose employee had issued a certificate of fitness for the vehicle after a carelessly inadequate test. The answer given was. *Yes*, so it was a fairly early instance of negligence liability in tort for economic loss. The stock criticism of the sort of thing there said is on the lines that it means uncertainty: it is not so much a principle, more a list of rather vague relevant considerations: it leaves too much to the particular Judge and the particular facts. A purpose of the present lecture is to see whether the 21 years have led to any significant tightening up or clarification. During that period my colleagues and I in New Zealand have repeated from time to time, possibly *ad nauseam* and certainly once with the endorsement of Lord Templeman for the Privy Council, essentially the same approach as was taken in that case decided in 1975, with a few attempted embellishments of the language.[11]

---

[8] Vol.28 (1994) at 821, *Courts and Torts: "Public Policy" Without Public Politics?*

[9] [1995] 2 A.C. 207; *Five Days in the House of Lords* (1995) 3 T.L.J. 169.

[10] *Rutherford v. Attorney-General* [1976] N.Z.L.R. 403, 411.

[11] See for example *Brown v. Heathcote County Council* [1986] 1 N.Z.L.R. 76, 79–80, C.A., [1987] 1 N.Z.L.R. 720, P.C. *South Pacific Manufacturing Co. Ltd v. New Zealand Security Investigations Ltd* [1992] 2 N.Z.L.R. 282, 293–4, 305–6, 312, 316–7, 324–5. The passage in *Brown* which the Privy Council described as useful is as follows—

" . . . we have considered first the degree of proximity and foreseeability of harm as between the parties. I would put it as whether these factors are strong enough to point prima facie to a duty of care. Second, if necessary, we have considered whether there are other particular factors pointing against a duty. It is also conceivable that other factors could strengthen the case for a duty. . . . we have found this kind of analysis helpful in determining whether it is just and reasonable that a duty of care of a particular scope was incumbent upon the defendant.

We have also recognised that, if the loss in question is merely economic, that may tell against a duty . . . [although] the economic loss point [is not] automatically fatal to a duty of care."

THE SIGNIFICANCE OF HEDLEY BYRNE

At Oxford in 1993, at the behest of Professor Peter Birks and for one of the Society of Public Teachers of Law seminars on *The Frontiers of Liability*,[12] I essayed an account of the condition of the law of tort. It was stretchingly extensive as to the subject-matter, although Tony Weir, in the course of letting off his concluding fireworks, complained[13] *inter alia* that it (like the other papers at the session) did not deal with defamation, a subject in which in fact I have had a number of immersions both at the bar and on the bench, but which can hardly be covered sensibly in a paragraph or two of a general discussion of tort law. When he has a day or two to spare, however, we could go through my defamation cases together.

On that occasion I thought tentatively to identify four major breakthrough cases in the development of civil liability law in England during the twentieth century. They were *Nocton v. Ashburton*[14], *Donoghue v. Stevenson*,[15] *Home Office v. Dorset Yacht Co. Ltd*,[16] and *United Scientific Holdings Ltd v. Burnley Borough Council*.[17] The latter case was included because of the authoritative recognition of the intermingling or fusion of law and equity by Lords Diplock and Simon of Glaisdale, whose speeches were in substance agreed with on this matter by the other three members of the House. On further reflection *Dorset Yacht* should be replaced on the list by *Hedley Byrne*. It is true that in its impact on the case in hand the actual decision of the House of Lords in *Hedley Byrne* was less important, for after all the lower courts were affirmed; but the *ratio decidendi* of all the Law Lords who sat—that there would have been a duty of care but for the disclaimer—represented a major advance in the law of England. As Lord Devlin's superbly constructed speech brought out, the decision was incremental (although he did not use that word and might have found it unhelpful), but it enunciated expressly for the first time that there may be a duty of care in tort to avoid causing purely economic damage.

[12] Vol.2, 49.
[13] *Ibid*. 103.
[14] [1914] A.C. 932.
[15] [1932] A.C. 562.
[16] [1970] A.C. 1004.
[17] [1978] A.C. 904.

That can indeed be seen as implicit in *Nocton v. Ashburton*, especially the speech of Lord Haldane L.C. The cardinal point of *Hedley Byrne*, however, is the explicit rejection of the argument for the respondent that, for negligence liability in tort, financial loss must flow from physical damage to the person or the property of the plaintiff. By comparison *Dorset Yacht*, although certainly important in extending duties of care somewhat into the field of public authority discretions, was rather easier. The damage to the yachts was physical. One may readily agree that nevertheless damage to chattels (or realty) is essentially economic loss to the plaintiff owners. Yet it can be said to be not "pure" economic loss. For the latter *Hedley Byrne* is the key authority.[18] That breakthrough made it much easier for the House of Lords to move, "incrementally" if you like, to such decisions as *Henderson v. Merrett Syndicates Ltd*[19] and *White & Jones*[20] recognising that duties of care not to cause such loss are naturally perfectly acceptable even if not based on particular statements made by the defendant or particular reliance by the plaintiff.

In these three cases the untidy complexity of life has indeed led the House of Lords to resist the temptation of elegance. Yielding to it would have been easy enough. To many legal minds of the past, and no doubt to some of the present, it is attractive to lay down that when two parties are in a contractual relationship there is no room for tort liability, and that purely economic loss occasioned by negligence is the exclusive business of the law of

[18] In the sea of writings on the significance of *Hedley Byrne* one of the outstanding landmarks remains the early article about the case by Robert Stevens in (1964) 27 M.L.R. 121. At 130, n.4, he mentions that the first House of Lords hearing began before an entirely differently constituted Appellate Committee, dominated by Chancery lawyers, but had to be abandoned because of Viscount Radcliffe's appointment to preside at the Vassal Tribunal. See also Blom-Cooper and Drewry *Final Appeal* (Clarendon Press, Oxford, 1972) 153, 293. I have been told that Gerald Gardiner Q.C., having encountered an apparently unsympathetic hearing on the first day, seized the opportunity of representing to the Lord Chancellor, Lord Dilhorne, that the fresh hearing should be before an Appellate Committee with more common lawyers. In the event Gardiner (who in the following year was to replace Dilhorne as Lord Chancellor) can thus be said to have achieved a victory for the progress of the common law, although not victory for his side in the particular case. He had not appeared in the courts below and it has been suggested that the disclaimer on which the claim foundered was always destined to be an awkward point for the appellants. But they had initially made a charge of fraud and despite abandoning this (see [1962] 1 Q.B. at 399) may well have felt strongly about the conduct of the respondents.

[19] [1995] 2 A.C. 145 (duties of insurance syndicate managing agents to members).

[20] [1995] 2 A.C. 207 (duties of solicitor to prospective beneficiaries of client's will).

contractual obligations. Simply, it has come to be perceived that these solutions are neither just, nor fair nor reasonable, which terms are of course overlapping and perhaps interchangeable.

PSEUDO CRITERIA

In the 21 years already mentioned there has been a deluge of relevant case law and academic writing in jurisdictions round the world. Has all this led to clearer criteria for negligence liability, tests more conducive to certainty? As to that, unfortunately, at least three negative factors have been at work.

First, I was wrong to include *proximity* in the guidelines. In a number of judgments and writings over the years I have in effect admitted this by pointing out that the term, which may have been first used in this field by A.L. Smith L.J. in *Le Lievre v. Gould*,[21] is only a label, a convenient way of announcing that the court has concluded that there is a sufficient connection between the defendant and the plaintiff to justify recognition of a duty of care. It is of course the closeness of their relations, not necessarily in the physical sense, which is referred to, as Lord Atkin himself pointed out in *Donoghue v. Stevenson*.[22] The term itself is currently much employed but gives no help at all in ascertaining whether the courts will regard the relationship as close enough. There is no need to labour the point by a multiplicity of citations. I can now cite simply Lord Nicholls of Birkenhead, who this year, in *Stovin v. Wise*,[23] has put it, after mentioning *Caparo Industries plc v Dickman*,[24]—

"The *Caparo* tripartite test elevates proximity to the dignity of a separate heading. This formulation tends to suggest that proximity is a separate ingredient, distinct from fairness and reasonableness, and capable of being identified by some other criteria. This is not so. Proximity is a slippery word. Proximity is not legal shorthand for a concept with its own, objectively identifiable characteristics. Proximity is convenient shorthand for a relationship between two parties which makes it fair

[21] [1893] 1 Q.B. 491, 504.
[22] [1932] A.C. at 581.
[23] [1996] A.C. at 923; [1996] 3 W.L.R. 388, 395; [1996] 3 All E.R. 801, 808. In the same case at 241 Lord Steyn says that he is willing to assume that there was a sufficient degree of proximity and that the crucial question therefore becomes whether it would be fair, just and reasonable to impose a duty of care. I am respectfully querying whether anything worthwhile is achieved by separating the questions.
[24] [1990] 2 A.C. 605, 617–8.

and reasonable that one should owe the other a duty of care. This is only another way of saying that when assessing the requirements of fairness and reasonableness regard must be had to the relationship of the parties."

In the sense, then, that it is of no value as a guide, *proximity* is a pseudo-criterion. The same is true, and almost as obviously, of another judicially "in" word, *incremental*. You may remember that one of my opening list of quotations pointed out the meaning of this word. It has been popular in legal usage in England since a use of it by Brennan J. in the High Court of Australia struck a chord in *Murphy v. Brentwood District Council*.[25]

In *Murphy* and like contexts there may be a tacit suggestion that an increment is only a *very little* addition; but, if so, this is as unsound etymologically as it would be if intended to reflect the way in which the common law has been developed. For instance, the precedents cited in the majority speeches in *Donoghue v. Stevenson* and *Dorset Yacht*, and in all the speeches in *Hedley Byrne*, provided solid logical justification for the major extensions of the common law made in those three cases. They were truly turning points of the common law. But at the same time they each had an impeccable pedigree; each was an addition to a well-established corpus. Lord Atkin, Lord Macmillan, Lord Reid, Lord Devlin and the others were making law incrementally.

That, too, was the function in which Lord Wilberforce saw himself engaged in his famous judgments in *Anns v. Merton London Borough Council*[26] and *McLoughlin v. O'Brian*.[27] The unconstructive attack on the first of these in particular might seem to be based on some failure of comprehension were it not for the undoubted usual acumen of the critics. In *Anns* Lord Wilberforce specifically founded on the earlier trilogy of cases in the House, saying before his two-stage proposition ". . . the position has now been reached . . .".[28] In *McLoughlin* he regarded the immediate aftermath

---

[25] [1991] 1 A.C. 398, 461, per Lord Keith of Kinkel, citing *Sutherland Shire Council v. Heyman* (1985) 157 C.L.R. 424, 481.

[26] [1975] A.C. 728.

[27] [1983] 1 A.C. 410.

[28] [1978] A.C. at 751. I have never believed that Lord Wilberforce was asserting that reasonable foresight alone is *prima facie* a ground for a duty of care. It is of course plain both from that speech and from what he said in *McLoughlin v. O'Brian* [1983] 1 A.C. 410, 420–1, that he was far from regarding foresight as automatically leading to a duty; but even as to the *prima facie* stage his wording in *Anns* need not be so read. In the end the point should not matter if one accepts that he had no intention whatever of a massive extension of duties of care. A weighing

psychiatric damage decisions as a logical extension of existing authority, demanded by justice.[29]

Clearly some Judges and other lawyers would not themselves have favoured the developments in the last five cases that I have cited. There may be some who would not have favoured any of them, some who would join Lord Buckmaster and Lord Tomlin in seeing the majority decision in *Donoghue v. Stevenson* as just as out of place in robust and commonsense England as the laws of Babylon.[30] Be that as it may, the additions made to the common law in the five cases were plainly intended by their architects to be incremental. Propounded as if it were a guide rather than a label, *incremental* should likewise be discarded as an unhelpful concept.

Thirdly, an unhappy degradation has occurred with *foresight*. In expositions of the law a habit has set in of categorising as not reasonably foreseeable occurrences which clearly are in fact so foreseeable, but which the court, desiring this result in the sense of the third of my listed quotations (from Lord Goff), decides to exclude from the scope of a duty of care. The Hillsborough disaster case, *Alcock v. Chief Constable of South Yorkshire Police*,[31] furnishes examples. Clearly it is reasonably foreseeable that in a large crowd at a sporting event there may be some, outside the categories of husband and wife and parent and child, who could well suffer psychiatric injury from seeing or fearing the death in any disaster of a loved one also present. Most of the speeches in that case appear to indicate, however, that the defendant will not be taken to have reasonably foreseen psychiatric injury to such claimants unless as regards each there is evidence, *ex post facto*, of a particularly close tie.[32]

Yet the defendant will know nothing of the actual circumstances and relationships of the vast majority of the crowd. Apart from a few cases of personal knowledge, the defendant's actual reasonable foresight will be no more than that spectators with varying relationships are at risk of (*inter alia*) psychiatric injury. To differentiate the defendant's duties of care according to the particular

process is of the essence of his approach, however his *Anns* proposition be interpreted. And be warned that I am about to plagiarise Horace. *Annsam expelles furca, tamen usque recurret.*

[29] [1983] 1 A.C. at 418–9 and 422–3.
[30] See [1932] A.C. at 578.
[31] [1992] 1 A.C. 310.
[32] See [1992] 1 A.C. at 397, 404, 422.

relationship that turns out in fact to have existed is to distort the notion of reasonable foresight. This is indeed brought out in several passages in the speech of Lord Oliver of Aylmerton.[33] So, too, it is in fact reasonably foreseeable that people watching a live television broadcast of a disaster may suffer trauma from knowledge that loved ones are at the place. The reasons for excluding television viewers from the ambit of the defendant's duty may or may not be good policy reasons. On analysis they are no more and no less than the floodgates argument. They have nothing to do with reasonable foresight.

RELIANCE AND ASSUMPTION OF RESPONSIBILITY

Happily the changes in the 21 years have not all been regressive. The law has moved forwards in identifying more clearly the twin notions of *reliance* (by the plaintiff) and *assumption of responsibility* (by the defendant) as aids in determining whether or not there is tort liability in negligence. From a slightly different perspective, both may be seen as results of the *control* of activities in a particular field, such as new housing certification, which at least the Canadian and New Zealand courts have regarded as important. The Privy Council has now sanctioned this for New Zealand, in relation to the housing cases, in *Invercargill City Council v. Hamlin*.[34] I do not propose to say anything here about the law of England in the field of housing. That field is one in which control and consequent assumption of responsibility by the certifying local authority is of a general social kind. The same applies to the implied assumption of responsibility of a developer who puts up houses for people to live in for many years. The local authority and the developer alike, by statute or choice respectively, each take on a role in the community naturally carrying with it a responsibility of exercising reasonable care.

That is different from and based on wider considerations than *Hedley Byrne* liability.[35] The latter is more case-specific. It derives from a voluntary assumption of responsibility more equivalent to

---

[33] *e.g.* at 410 and 418.
[34] [1996] A.C. 624, 638–9, *per* Lord Lloyd of Berwick.
[35] A point made more fully by Lord Hoffmann in *Stovin v. Wise* [1996] A.C. at 923.

contract, as Lord Devlin said.[36] It was more naturally applied by Lord Goff of Chieveley in *Henderson v. Merrett Syndicates Ltd*,[37] a case which, because it marked the final acceptance in England that a duty may arise, between the same parties and in the same circumstances, from both tort and contract, rivalled *Hedley Byrne* when I was vacillating over which English tort case to take as one of the Turning Points for this series of lectures.

It seems to me strange that some scholars of high repute have criticised the theoretical basis of *Hedley Byrne*. We know that the origins of the "modern" law of informal contracts lay in the old tort action of assumpsit. And Lord Lloyd is surely right in saying, after referring to *Henderson v. Merrett Syndicates Ltd*, "The House rejected an approach which treated the law of tort as supplementary to the law of contract, i.e. as providing for a tortious remedy only where there is no contract. On the contrary: the law of tort is the general law, out of which the parties may, if they can, contract."[38] When there arises a new category of case involving assumption of responsibility, once it is accepted that the justice of the case and any other relevant considerations require a remedy, why try to force the case into a contractual mould instead of the more flexible general law? No doubt the concept of consideration could be extended, albeit not altogether easily; but to do so would be to add unnecessary technicality to what should be a straightforward subject.

I must own to slightly more sympathy, however, for the suggestion that there is also something artificial about the way in which the more specific kind of assumption of responsibility was stretched in the House of Lords in *White v. Jones*.[39] This is not to associate myself with a comparison with the heel of Achilles. I think that a solution by way of extending contract law would have been equally artificial. The contract made by the solicitor when he took instructions to prepare a will for his client was not to confer a benefit on a third party, but to enable the client to do so. In *Gartside v. Sheffield, Young & Ellis*,[40] decided in New Zealand 12

---

[36] [1964] A.C. at 525–30. Robert Stevens argued in the article cited in n.18 *supra* that the historical concept of warranty should have been utilised. An unconscious echo of that approach may be found in an article entitled *An Impossible Distinction* in (1991) 107 L.Q.R. 46.

[37] [1995] 2 A.C. 145.

[38] *Marc Rich & Co. A.G. v. Bishop Rock Marine Co. Ltd* [1996] 1 A.C. 211, 223.

[39] [1995] 2 A.C. 207.

[40] [1983] N.Z.L.R. 37.

years before *White v. Jones* and on facts assumed at the pre-trial stage to be materially identical with those on which that case came to be decided, we reached the same result with no more than a passing reference in one of the judgments to *Hedley Byrne*.[41] The case was seen rather as one of the general responsibility of solicitors carrying on their profession in the community. It is gratifying that Lord Goff was prepared to accept that this is at least among the reasons why to allow an intended beneficiary a remedy for the solicitor's dilatoriness gives effect to what his Lordship calls "... the strong impulse for practical justice".[42] After all, practical justice is what the law of negligence is for. It needs no other justification.

Practical justice of course may not be high on the list of priorities of insurance companies. In his survey of Commonwealth case law in *White v. Jones* Lord Goff mentions the varying Australian decisions, including that of the Supreme Court of Victoria in *Seale v. Perry*[43] which, reversing Anderson J., was against a duty of care to intended beneficiaries. I understand that an appeal by the plaintiff to the High Court of Australia was stopped by payment to the plaintiff of the full amount of the first instance judgment. The precedent of the decision at State appellate level was thus preserved, at least for the time being.

THE POSITION TODAY

In *Marc Rich & Co. v. Bishop Rock Marine Co. Ltd*[44] Lord Steyn, with the concurrence of three other Law Lords, has said:

> "Counsel for the cargo owners submitted that in cases of physical damage to property in which the plaintiff has a proprietary or possessory interest the only requirement is proof of reasonable foreseeability. For this proposition he relied on observations of Lord Oliver of Aylmerton in *Caparo Industries Plc. v. Dickman*.[45] Those observations, seen in context, do not support his argument. They merely underline the qualitative difference between cases of direct physical damage and

---

[41] *Ibid*. 46, where Richardson J. made it clear that he was not applying the "separate *Hedley Byrne* duty approach."

[42] [1995] 2 A.C. at 260.

[43] [1982] V.R. 193.

[44] [1996] 1 A.C. 211, 235–6.

[45] [1990] 2 A.C. 605, 632C-633D.

indirect economic loss. The materiality of that distinction is plain. But since the decision in *Dorset Yacht Co. Ltd v. Home Office*[46] it has been settled law that the elements of foreseeability and proximity as well as considerations of fairness, justice and reasonableness are relevant to all cases whatever the nature of the harm sustained by the plaintiff. Saville L.J. explained:[47]

> '... whatever the nature of the harm sustained by the plaintiff, it is necessary to consider the matter not only by inquiring about fore-seeability but also by considering the nature of the relationship between the parties; and to be satisfied that in all the circumstances it is fair, just and reasonable to impose a duty of care. Of course, ..., these three matters overlap with each other and are really facets of the same thing. For example, the relationship between the parties may be such that it is obvious that a lack of care will create a risk of harm and that as a matter of common sense and justice a duty should be imposed ... Again in most cases of the direct infliction of physical loss or injury through carelessness, it is self-evident that a civilised system of law should hold that a duty of care has been broken, whereas the infliction of financial harm may well pose a more difficult problem. Thus the three so-called requirements for a duty of care are not to be treated as wholly separate and distinct requirements but rather as convenient and helpful approaches to the pragmatic question whether a duty should be imposed in any given case. In the end whether the law does impose a duty in any particular circumstances depends upon those circumstances, ...'

That seems to me a correct summary of the law as it now stands. It follows that I would reject the first argument of counsel for the cargo owners."

Plus ça change ... Although rather fuller and incomparably more authoritative, that passage seems to be to much the same effect as my own rough shot at a generalisation when sitting at first instance 21 years ago. This branch of the law remains, as Lord Keith of Kinkel has said, intensely pragmatic.[48] Of course there is some uncertainty. The common law is always uncertain at the edges. As far as I know, it has never been demonstrated that there is less litigation in judicial climates where certainty is held up as a priceless asset, a god, than in those where a more liberal approach prevails for the time being. Bad law makes not only hard cases,

[46] [1970] A.C. 1004.
[47] At 1077D-E.
[48] *Rowling v. Takaro Properties Ltd* [1988] A.C. 473, 501.

but at least as many cases as law which does better justice.

The legitimate differences of opinion that can arise are perfectly illustrated, to take English examples, by the recent House of Lords cases of *Marc Rich*[49] and *Stovin v. Wise.*[50] In the first (no duty of care owed by classification society to cargo owners) Judges with the commercial law experience of Hirst J. and Lord Lloyd differed from a total of seven others. In the second (no duty of care on highway authority to expedite a road safety project) the respondent in the House had the galling experience of commanding preponderant judicial support by six to three but losing because the three constituted a majority of the House of Lords. Nothing would be gained by my entering the lists as to the actual decision in either case. But, having sinned myself in the *South Pacific Manufacturing* case[51] by failing to comply with the duty to avoid prolixity which falls on anyone discussing negligence in abstract terms, I will take the liberty of making two comments on *Stovin v. Wise.* The length of the discussion is aggravated by an inevitable guardedness that diminishes its impact, yet basically the issue may have been simply whether the council's employees were actionably negligent in allowing a project to go to sleep. And the way in which the House divided is a reminder of how much power can be exercised by those who select the Judges to sit in a particular case.

In evolving negligence law, as with the common law as a whole, courts can be much influenced by and seek to march with the general policy of Parliament.[52] Subject to that, the concepts, criteria and signposts have to be worked out by the Judges. Hans Linde's insistence on some identifiable external source goes, I think, too far. Remorselessly applied, it could mean that there would be hardly any common law at all. Notwithstanding the powerful arguments for state compensation for personal injuries, the New Zealand experience has been that, because of the cost to public funds, the scope of the scheme has to be restricted. In that field, although expelled by a pitchfork, the common law creeps back. In the field of economic injuries cautious evolution continues. By no means do these developments imply that the common law is automatically expansive. Progress does not consist simply in

---

[49] [1996] 1 A.C. 211.

[50] [1996] A.C. at 923; [1996] 3 W.L.R. 388; [1996] 3 All E.R. 801.

[51] [1992] 2 N.Z.L.R. 282.

[52] See the authorities collected in the *South Pacific Manufacturing* case, *cit.supra*, at 298.

giving judgment for the plaintiff. What is true is that the Judges have always had a creative role—indeed a duty. Some of the constitutional implications will be for Oxford next week. In the area of civil liability, as *Hedley Byrne* demonstrates, the Judges cannot discharge that duty without from time to time modifying and even jettisoning tenets that had seemed hallowed. The untidiness of life is forever overruling elegance.

Third Hamlyn Lecture
November 21, 1996
University of Cambridge

The Liberation of English Public Law

"... the landmark decision of this House in *Anisminic Ltd v. Foreign Compensation Commission* [1969] 2 A.C. 147, and particularly the leading speech of Lord Reid, ... has liberated English public law from the fetters that the courts had theretofore imposed upon themselves so far as determinations of inferior courts and statutory tribunals were concerned, by drawing esoteric distinctions between errors of law committed by such tribunals that went to their jurisdiction, and errors of law committed by them within their jurisdiction. The breakthrough that the *Anisminic* case made was the recognition by the majority of this House that if a tribunal whose jurisdiction was limited by statute or subordinate legislation mistook the law applicable to the facts as it had found them, it must have asked itself the wrong question, i.e., one into which it was not empowered to inquire and so had no jurisdiction to determine. Its purported "determination," not being a "determination" within the meaning of the empowering legislation, was accordingly a nullity."

O'Reilly v. Mackman [1983] 2 A.C. 237, 278, *per* Lord Diplock.

Before beginning this lecture mention should perhaps be made of the fact that in one respect it is unusual, in that advance notice of it appears to have been given in *The Times* crossword. On November 26, 1996 a number of clues yielded answers revealing the identity of the lecturer, the place and the subject. Inquiries into this matter are being pursued.

Last I come to the most important of all the four cases which I have selected as Turning Points of the Common Law. The most important because it has a constitutional dimension of the profoundest kind. It is unnecessary to know what has been said in any of the preceding three lectures. The Cambridge philosopher Wittgenstein in one of the few of his propositions intelligible to most of us without explanation laid down that "What can be said at all can be said clearly; and whereof one cannot speak thereof one must be silent." Few in this audience will have been at any of the first three lectures, none (I am confident) at all of them, so at the reception due to begin a short hour ahead most of those present will be easily able to comply with the second limb of Wittgenstein's injunction. On the other hand, in a field with an overlay of the esoteric I may be hard put to it to observe the first.

The text for the lecture has been taken from Lord Diplock, who as Diplock L.J. had given the longest of three judgments delivered in the Court of Appeal in *Anisminic*[1] in a unanimous decision that was reversed by the House of Lords. That was not the only major administrative law case in which a judgment of Diplock L.J. suffered such a fate. Another was *Padfield v. Minister of Agriculture*,[2] where the House of Lords held that a Minister must reconsider a complaint which he had rejected apparently for reasons of political expediency rather than reasons promoting the policy of the Act conferring his discretion. Diplock's *Padfield* and *Anisminic* judgments were in the years 1966 and 1967 when he was a senior Lord Justice of Appeal and shortly before his appointment (in 1968) as a Lord of Appeal in Ordinary. After some 12 years service in the Lords, and by now occupying the chair in the Appellate Committee, he made a generous and skilful judicial volte-face, embracing and ultimately even extending *Anisminic*, first hailing it as a legal landmark in 1980.[3] Two years later, in the case from which my text is taken, he described *Padfield* as "another case in which

[1] *Anisminic Ltd v. Foreign Compensation Commission* [1968] 2 Q.B. 862.
[2] [1968] A.C. 997, a report including the Court of Appeal judgments. Diplock and Russell L.JJ. constituted a majority. The result reached by Denning M.R., in a dissenting judgment, and at first instance by a Divisional Court headed by Lord Parker C.J., was preferred by a majority of four Law Lords (Lords Reid, Hodson, Pearce and Upjohn) to one (Lord Morris of Borth-y-Gest). It is noteworthy as illustrative of judicial approaches to administrative law that in both that case and *Anisminic* Lord Reid and Lord Pearce were in the "interventionist" majority, whereas in both Lord Morris dissented. Morris was a developer of the law of tort (*Hedley Byrne* and *Dorset Yacht*) but more cautious in public law, although he was a party to the Court of Appeal decision in *R. v. Northumberland Compensation Appeal Tribunal, ex p. Shaw* [1952] 1 K.B. 338 that the old remedy of certiorari for error of law on the face of the record applied to statutory tribunals. In *Anisminic* [1969] 2 A.C. at 183 he was, not surprisingly, impressed with the point that the *Northumberland* judgments would have been unnecessary if it could have been asserted that error of construction was tantamount to excess of jurisdiction. This did not trouble any of the other Law Lords or Lords Justices in *Anisminic*, none of whom had been in *Northumberland*. The latter was seen as a landmark case in its day. Listening to the arguments in the Court of Appeal was a highlight of my time as a research student at Cambridge. I recollect how effectively Gerald Gardiner K.C. made the point that judicial review on questions of law was appropriate, by beginning his argument by simply reading to the Court the Regulations which the Tribunal had to apply.
[3] *Re a Company* [1981] A.C. 374, 382, a case otherwise known as *Racal*.

a too timid judgment of my own in the Court of Appeal was (fortunately) overruled."[4]

LORD DIPLOCK AND HIS POSSIBLE FORMER FALLACY

A purist might say that all Judges are strictly unique, but Diplock's judicial writing has an unremittingly cerebral quality which makes it at times the very quintessence of uniqueness. The clarity recommended by Wittgenstein is generally thought to entail simplicity. For most purposes of comprehension it is preferable to be told that a transistor is an electronic switch rather than to be overwhelmed by precise analysis. That was not typically Diplock's way, more Denning's, but it happens that the elaboration in Diplock's reversed judgment in *Anisminic*, as well as being a prime example of his style, does expose its own weak point as a more superficial treatment of the subject would not. And this becomes highly relevant to an understanding of the true implications of *Anisminic* as later decided by the House of Lords. To preserve some show of clarity and simplicity, I will, however, relegate the central part of his exposition—and it is only the central part, there is much more in the same vein—to a very long footnote in the printed text of this lecture.[5] The length of the footnote can be

---

[4] [1983] 2 A.C. at 280.
[5] "The authority or 'jurisdiction' to determine whether a situation of a kind described in a statute exists is limited in a number of respects:

(1) The person or persons by whom it is exercised must possess the qualifications laid down in the statute. In addition, unless it is otherwise provided in the statute either expressly or by necessary implication, the presumed intention of Parliament is that one of the qualifications is absence of bias.

(2) The determination must be preceded by inquiry. The nature of the inquiry, any conditions precedent to the inquiry, and the procedure to be adopted in the inquiry, may be laid down expressly in the statute. In the absence of express provision to the contrary, the presumed intention of Parliament is that the inquiry shall be conducted in accordance with the rules of natural justice. A convenient summary of the relevant rules is to be found in the speech of Lord Loreburn L.C. in *Board of Education v. Rice.* [1911] A.C. 179.

(3) The case in which the determination is made must be one of the kind described in the statute. The statute may define the kind of cases which it confers authority upon a person to determine in a number of different ways. The description will necessarily include words identifying the person or class of persons who are entitled to initiate the inquiry leading to the deter-

---

defended only on the ground that the labyrinth into which Diplock's matchless analytical skills drove him shows that critics of the House of Lords decision do not necessarily have all the logic on their side, as they sometimes allege. A rough paraphrase of Diplock's reasoning in the Court of Appeal will have to do for this audience for the time being.

It was said by an Emeritus Fellow of this College about the definitive edition of Evelyn's Diary that the commentary "illuminated the dark places while refusing to lavish superfluous enlightenment on the obvious."[6] Diplock's analysis does illuminate dark places, but not, I suggest, in quite the way he intended. Roughly, what he appears to be saying is that, as to the reviewability on jurisdictional grounds of a decision of an inferior tribunal, the acid

> mination, and probably the other person or class of persons (if any) who are entitled to be parties to the inquiry. It will also necessarily contain a description of the subject-matter of the determination, that is, of the kind of dispute or claim to be determined.
>
> (4) The determination must state whether a situation of the kind described in the Act exists or not in the case of the individual to whom the determination relates.
>
> If any of these conditions is not complied with, the statement is not a 'determination' within the authority conferred by the statute, and effect will not be given to it by the executive branch of Government.
>
> The person authorised to make the determination must necessarily form an opinion as to whether each of those conditions is complied with, in order to embark upon and to proceed with the inquiry and to make the determination; but his opinion as to whether they are or not is not one to which effect will be given by the executive branch of Government. If it is 'wrong' in the opinion of a person to whose opinion as to whether or not any of the conditions are complied with effect will be given by the executive branch of Government, the error is an 'error going to the jurisdiction' of the inferior tribunal, and the purported determination is a nullity. This is not the substitution of the opinion of one person to whose opinion effect will be given for that of another to whose opinion effect would have been given but for such substitution. It is the first statement of any opinion to which effect will be given by the executive branch of Government. This is what distinguishes it from the case of a determination made where all these conditions are complied with, and to which effect would be given by the executive branch of Government but for the fact that the determination contains a statement as to the legal consequences of particular facts which in the opinion of the maker exist, and such statement is 'wrong' in the opinion of some other person to whose substituted opinion as to the legal consequences of particular facts effect will be given by the executive branch of Government. The error is then an 'error within jurisdiction'." [1968] 2 Q.B. at 890–1.

[6] J S G Simmons, Obituary of Esmond de Beer, *The Times* October 15, 1990.

test is whether the opinion of that tribunal, in the absence of any appeal, would be given effect by the Executive. And that there are four categories of cases, and only four, in which the Executive will not or should not give effect to the tribunal's opinions. These exceptional categories include opinions as to whether a given case is of a kind with which the legislation intends the tribunal to deal.

Penetrating though the analysis may seem, it reveals itself as based on assertions. Usually the Executive will enforce a decision of a tribunal unless a higher court or tribunal rules otherwise: surely this can be no test of jurisdiction. Then, more fundamentally, an opinion of a tribunal that a case is of the kind committed to it is not intrinsically different from any other opinion of the tribunal. It is just as necessary, for instance, for a tribunal to decide (a) whether a claimant qualifies for any benefit and (b) which of a range of benefits applies to the case. If the legislation can be held to authorise the tribunal to determine (b) conclusively, including any incidental questions of law, there is no inherent reason why it cannot be held to do the same as to (a). Again, if the governing legislation requires a claimant to be a British national, this may entail in some cases decisions of questions of law no less difficult and no less important than the question whether the legislation requires any successor in title to the claimant to be a British national as well. Of course these various questions are different; but there is no natural distinction putting some of them within the tribunal's jurisdiction, field or area, for the purposes of judicial review, and some outside it.

TEMPS PERDU

Forty years and more ago I undertook research for a Ph.D degree at another university. Against all advice, the subject chosen was *Jurisdiction*. The theme of the present series of lectures may suggest that the weakness of an inclination to plunge unnecessarily into a huge sea of troubles has never been shaken off. The dissertation, for such they are called there, was to be published by the university press, but required conversion. I have been busy since and have not got round to it. Also *Anisminic* has solved a number of the problems with which the young researcher struggled, by selecting for the law of England a path that was certainly among those open in the early nineteen fifties but could just as easily not have been preferred.[7] Also one had a suspicion that the truth was such as it would have been presumptuous for a very junior academic of those days to state openly. Nowadays there appear to be no such inhibitions among academics at any level. It was perhaps not until 1978 that complete candour in this particular matter was thought judicially appropriate, and then Lord Denning indulged in a little irony. He said that so fine is the distinction that in truth the High Court has a choice before it whether to interfere with an inferior court on a point of law. "Softly be it stated, but that is the reason for the difference between the decision of the Court of Appeal in *Anisminic* ... and the House of Lords."[8]

Softly be it added that those observations are also a little exaggerated. The subject does lend itself to alternative approaches, but they are alternatives of logic or principle, not a mere discretionary morass. This may conveniently be brought out by taking the facts of *Anisminic* itself.

One preliminary point has to be mentioned. Sometimes the issue is intertwined with statutory provisions of varying wording but generally in the nature of privative, ouster, no certiorari or finality clauses. I shall call them all simply privative clauses. They are much less common in England today, because in relation to tribunals which are not courts of law they are effectively excluded from Acts passed before August 1, 1958 by provisions now appearing in section 12 of the Tribunals and Inquiries Act 1992. Because of the manner in which privative clauses are habitually interpreted, the notes to section 12 in 10 Halsbury's Statutes (4th edition, 1995 Reissue, 483), express a common understanding in the legal profession by saying that at least in England and Wales the section is "not of much practical importance." There was a privative clause in *Anisminic*, as the Tribunals and Inquiries Act 1958, s.11, corresponding to the current s.12, expressly exempted the Foreign Compensation Commission. There was also a privative clause in the current somewhat controversial case of *R. v.*

---

[7] Leading cases that could be seen to point another way included *R. v. Bolton* (1841) 1 Q.B. 66, *R. v. Nat Bell Liquors Ltd* [1922] 2 A.C. 128, and *R. v. Northumberland Compensation Appeal Tribunal*, cit. *supra*—all indicating that jurisdiction was fixed at the inception of a hearing or an inquiry and not lost by an error of law in the course of it (provided, presumably, that the ultimate order was one which the supervising court considered that the tribunal had power to make): all treating as crucial the face of the record, an illogical concept yet abundantly supported by authority.

[8] *Pearlman v. Keepers and Governors of Harrow School* [1979] 1 Q.B. 56, 70.

Secretary of State for the Home Department, ex p. Fayed[9] on which, as it may still be in a sense sub judice, it will not be prudent for me to comment. In neither case did the clause affect the result, although as to *Fayed* one must add "so far".

Turning, then, to *Anisminic*, the real issue was whether a claim to participate in a compensation fund received after Suez by the United Kingdom Government from the Egyptian Government was barred by the fact that the claimant company, whose Egyptian property had been sequestrated, had thereafter sold the property to an Egyptian organisation for the best price it could get in the circumstances, albeit much less than its actual value. The settlement expressly excluded any claim that the company might have against any governmental authority other than the Egyptian Government. The Foreign Compensation Commission had the function of determining claims on the fund in accordance with a complex Order in Council. They found that the company did not qualify as a claimant. I have said "the real issue"; but the importance of another issue, that of ensuring in the interests of justice that tribunals give reasons for their decisions, is underlined by the course of the case. Originally no reasons were available to the company. By a skilled use of correspondence and the process of discovery in an action for a declaration, the company's professional advisers elicited the reasons.[10]

The key point in the reasons was that, in the Commission's view, to qualify for compensation the company would have had to show that, not only was it a British national (which happened to be clear), but also that any successor in title to it was a British national (which equally clearly the transferee Egyptian organisation was not). Whether this was the "true" interpretation of the Order in Council was the crux of the argument, "true" being an adjective

---

[9] [1997] 1 All E.R. 228.

[10] The names of Roger Parker Q.C. and Patrick Neill Q.C., who represented the company throughout the court proceedings, should be recorded here. It was a case with distinguished counsel. The Commission were represented in the Court of Appeal (where they won without difficulty) by Sydney Templeman Q.C., Nigel Bridge and Christopher Cochrane. In the House of Lords, Gordon Slynn was their second counsel (Bridge J., as he then was, having been appointed to the bench). I have authority to record the following generous verdict. Lord Templeman's opinion is that in rejecting his arguments the House of Lords, and especially Lord Reid, "got it right": that they made a policy decision open to them on the previous authorities and in the best interests of the future of administrative law.

customarily used by Judges to denote the interpretation which they prefer.

For the purposes of judicial review, including an action for a declaration as in *Anisminic*,[11] four possible solutions for the *Anisminic* type problem compete.

ALTERNATIVE PATHS

(i)   It can be said that the jurisdiction of the tribunal is to be ascertained at (or perhaps about) the commencement of its inquiry and by the kind of order which it ultimately makes. The tribunal must also comply with the rules of natural justice regarding a fair hearing and freedom from bias. Provided that it complies with these limitations, questions of interpretation and other questions of law arising in the course of its proceedings and decision are conclusively the function of the tribunal itself, and beyond attack in the superior courts. This is what in *Anisminic* Lord Reid called the narrow and original sense of "jurisdiction".[12] Looked at from another angle, it is the sense of that term giving the tribunal probably the widest practicable immunity from judicial review. Privative clauses fall neatly into place, even if largely unnecessary. Such clauses would not be expected to cover a purported determination reached quite outside the tribunal's field or by a procedure contrary to natural justice.

Though logical enough, the foregoing approach does leave some grey areas. For instance, Who has the last word on whether a given party comes within the tribunal's jurisdiction? And, if there is an error of law on the face of the record, can that error be corrected by a reviewing court and does it make any difference whether or not there is a privative clause?

Note that in *Anisminic* Lord Morris adopted the foregoing approach, accepting however that the error-on-the-face jurisdiction would still apply but only if there was no privative clause.[13] It is an approach with very respectable antecedents, although the face-of-the-record exception weakens it. For, if evi-

---

[11] The procedural tangle in which English administrative law became enmeshed, after amendments to R.S.C. O.53 and Lord Diplock's exposition in *O'Reilly v. Mackman* of a dichotomy dividing public law and private law, is outside the scope of this lecture. *Public Law* has been adopted in the present era as a convenient rubric, but perhaps is no more than that.

[12] [1969] 2 A.C. at 171.

[13] *Ibid*. 183.

dence shows beyond a peradventure that the tribunal has made what the court regards as a mistake of law, why in this day and age should it matter whether technically the error is or is not disclosed by the record? The best argument for the approach is that developed by Lord Morris. In the course of a tribunal's deliberations a host of questions of law can arise: it can be most difficult to distinguish some kinds of questions from others: therefore only questions beyond very wide boundaries should be treated as outside the tribunal's field.

(ii)   Nevertheless the first approach does recognise some boundaries. It should not be overlooked, though, that this is not logically inevitable. There is no logical reason (but I shall suggest later that there is a constitutional one) why the legislature, while intending a tribunal to operate in a limited field, should not nevertheless allow the tribunal itself to determine conclusively whether cases fall within that field. Indeed that is the position of superior courts of general jurisdiction, such as in England the High Court of Justice. In national domestic law such courts determine conclusively the limits of their own jurisdiction, subject only to any right of appeal that may exist. A decision of such a court, express or implied, is never a nullity, as Salmond J. pointed out long ago.[14] Distinguished Judges have sometimes overlooked this, or at least have used language suggesting that they have done so, but now it is well accepted.[15]

Parliament might conceivably, probably unthinkingly, try to put a limited tribunal in the same position. As Lord Wilberforce said in *Anisminic*,[16] "Although in theory perhaps it may be possible for Parliament to set up a tribunal which has full and autonomous powers to fix its own area of operation, that has, so far, not been done in this country." We will do well to note the caution with which this proposition is worded. Later in his speech his Lordship cites a passage from Farwell L.J., calling it "language which, though perhaps vulnerable to logical analysis, has proved its value as guidance to the courts".[17] The passage includes "... it is a contradiction in terms to create a tribunal with limited jurisdiction and unlimited power to determine such limit at its own will and

---

[14]   *New Zealand Waterside Workers' Federation v. Frazer* [1924] N.Z.L.R. 689, 706–7. See *Venire de Novo* (1955) 71 L.Q.R. 100, 117, n.28.

[15]   *Re a Company* [1981] A.C. 374, 384, *per* Lord Diplock.

[16]   [1969] 2 A.C. at 207.

[17]   *Ibid*. 208.

pleasure—such a tribunal would be autocratic, not limited ...".[18]
These are deep-rooted sentiments. The extreme hands-off
approach is never likely to be accepted by any English court or
any court in the former Dominions.

(iii) The solution adopted by the majority Law Lords in *Anisminic*, including Lord Pearson who dissented only on the "true"
interpretation of the successor-in-title provisions, might be understood to be, if one looked only at what they themselves actually
said in their speeches, that there are some questions of law arising
in the course of a tribunal decision on which its decision will not
be vulnerable (unless perhaps the alleged error is apparent on the
face of the record) but others so arising which are open to review
on jurisdictional grounds.

As regards the latter the tribunal is held to go outside its field
or area, or exceed or fail to exercise its jurisdiction, if it *asks itself
the wrong question*; as, for example, by failing to take into account
something which, on the reviewing court's interpretation, it was
required to take into account, or basing its decision on some matter
which, again on the reviewing court's interpretation, it had no
right to take into account. This is a summary more particularly of
the speech of Lord Reid. On this approach—or the approach in (i)
above—the privative clause does not apply, for the determination
is not the kind of determination which the legislation set out to
protect. It was into the category of asking the wrong question that
the tribunal's decision in *Anisminic* was held by the House of
Lords to fall. On the "true" interpretation the Order in Council
required the Commission to be satisfied that the claimant company
was a British national and was at the time of the seizure the owner
of the relevant property in Egypt. The Commission, through what
three of their Lordships thought a misinterpretation, had imposed
a further condition precedent: namely that the successor in title
(the Egyptian organisation), although not a claimant, must also be
a British national. That "went to jurisdiction."

Lord Reid's speech has become the classic exposition of this
kind of solution. It was in its own way as Saul-like a transformation
as that of Lord Diplock when he became converted to the liberation
of administrative law quite late in his judicial career. Observers of
Lord Reid from more angles than one could not fail to see that
during the argument in the House of Lords, spread over 12 days,

[18] *R. v. Shoreditch Assessment Committee, ex p. Morgan* [1910] 2 K.B. 859, 880.

at some stage he changed his mind. Starting from what one observer has unkindly called a strict Scottish approach (which would have led him down the same path as his eminent Welsh colleague), he moved perceptibly to a more liberal position. He made no secret of this, and is known to have given *Anisminic* as an instance of the value of oral argument.

I have to point out that the majority Law Lords in *Anisminic* did appear to accept plainly enough that there would still be some questions of law, or involving law, on which in any given case the Tribunal would have a power of conclusive ruling. Thus Lord Reid said "If the commission were entitled to enter on the inquiry whether the applicants had a successor in title, then their decision as to whether T.E.D.O. was their successor in title would I think be unassailable whether it was right or wrong . . .".[19] Lords Pearce, Wilberforce and Pearson spoke to the same effect.[20] That is not to say, however, that these opinions represented unalterable positions on an issue which, strictly, they did not have to decide. The history of modern English administrative law has been one of evolution.[21] We must not assume that under prompting from Lord Diplock the majority in *Anisminic* would not, in due course, have been prepared to go further.

(iv)   There remains the fourth solution, which is almost at the end of the spectrum furthest from the second, and which belongs to Lord Diplock. He was not a member of the Appellate Committee in *Anisminic*, but, as I have heard a Law Lord who was a member put it, he ran away with the case. This appropriation began in *Racal* and was finally accomplished in *O'Reilly v. Mackman* in the passage taken as the text for this lecture. It will be apparent that, possibly with a degree of daring and certainly with a coup de maître, he extended *Anisminic* by treating the reasoning there as having abolished, as regards inferior courts and statutory tribunals, what he justly called the esoteric distinctions between errors of law going to jurisdiction and errors of law within jurisdiction. One is driven into French for emphasis. It is important to bear in mind that the other four members of the Appellate

---

[19] [1969] 2 A.C. at 174.
[20] *Ibid.* 195, 205, 207, 209 *et seq.*, 215.
[21] See *R. v. Bedwellty Justices, ex p. Williams* [1996] 3 W.L.R. 361, 367–8; [1996] 3 All E.R. 737, 743–5, and the citations there, including references to the standard text books Wade and Forsyth, and De Smith, Woolf and Jowell.

Committee in *O'Reilly v. Mackman* agreed with Lord Diplock's speech without qualification.

And, subject only to two qualifications, the Diplock principle as to this matter has become an orthodoxy. Thus in *R. v. Hull University Visitor, ex p. Page*[22] the five members of the House of Lords were unanimous as to the general principle. Lord Griffiths:[23]

> "It is in my opinion important to keep the purpose of judicial review clearly in mind. The purpose is to ensure that those bodies that are susceptible to judicial review have carried out their public duties in the way it was intended they should. In the case of bodies other than courts, in so far as they are required to apply the law they are required to apply the law correctly. If they apply the law incorrectly they have not performed their duty correctly and judicial review is available to correct their error of law so that they may make their decision upon a proper understanding of the law.
>
> In the case of inferior courts, that is, courts of a lower status than the High Court, such as the justices of the peace, it was recognised that their learning and understanding of the law might sometimes be imperfect and require correction by the High Court and so the rule evolved that certiorari was available to correct an error of law of an inferior court. At first it was confined to an error on the face of the record but it is now available to correct any error of law made by an inferior court."

Lord Browne-Wilkinson with the concurrence of Lord Keith of Kinkel:[24]

> "In my judgment the decision in *Anisminic Ltd v. Foreign Compensation Commission* [1969] 2 A.C. 147 rendered obsolete the distinction between errors of law on the face of the record and other errors of law by extending the doctrine of *ultra vires*. Thenceforward it was to be taken that Parliament had only conferred the decision-making power on the basis that it was to be exercised on the correct legal basis: a misdirection in law in making the decision therefore rendered the decision ultra vires. Professor Wade considers that the true effect of *Anisminic* is still in doubt: *Administrative Law*, 6th ed., pp. 299 *et seq*. But in my judgment the decision of this House in *O'Reilly v. Mackman* [1983] 2 A.C. 237 establishes the law in the sense that I have stated."

[22] [1993] A.C. 682.
[23] *Ibid*. 693.
[24] *Ibid*. 701.

Lord Slynn of Hadley with the concurrence of Lord Mustill, simply:[25]

"I accordingly accept that certiorari is now available to quash errors of law in a decision."

As to the two qualifications, one relates to the 'peculiar or domestic law' which is said to be within the exclusive jurisdiction of a university visitor, and possibly also, to some extent, wholly distinct areas of law such as the systems administered by ecclesiastical courts and military courts.[26] At first sight, looking at *Page's* case itself, it might be thought that the English courts would be prepared to review decisions relating to staff contracts and non-arcane university statutes; but philosophobia has proved a powerful deterrent. As Lord Griffiths observed in *Page*, "The learning and ingenuity of those members of the foundation who are likely to be in dispute with the foundation should not be lightly underestimated . . ."[27]

The second qualification relates to privative clauses. In the *Racal* case[28] Lord Diplock recognised a difference between administrative tribunals and authorities on the one hand and inferior courts of law on the other. He treated *Anisminic* in its full force as applicable only to the administrative bodies. I doubt whether Lord Reid had intended to make any material distinction,[29] but that

---

[25] *Ibid.* 706.

[26] Nonetheless these courts are undoubtedly amenable to some degree of judicial review: *R. v. Chancellor of St Edmundsbury and Ipswich Diocese, ex p. White* [1948] 1 K.B. 195, 207, 219 (prohibition but not *certiorari* lies to an ecclesiastical court); *Close v. Maxwell* [1945] N.Z.L.R. 688 (*certiorari* and prohibition against court martial: desertion not established by mere refusal to attend embarkation parade). See also *James v. London & South Western Railway Co.* (1872) L.R. 7 Ex. 287 (prohibition to Court of Admiralty). Although jurisdiction in admiralty was later transferred to the High Court, the *James* case has some continuing importance, because it recognises that a court can be entitled to be designated a superior court, yet be of limited jurisdiction and therefore amenable to prohibition. It was only superior courts of general jurisdiction that were outside control by the prerogative writs.

[27] [1993] A.C. at 694.

[28] *Re a Company* [1981] A.C. 374, 382–3.

[29] See his reference in [1969] 2 A.C. at 171 to *R. v. Governor of Brixton Prison, ex p. Armah* [1968] A.C. 192, 234, where he had spoken in an undifferentiating way of "a magistrate or any other tribunal". *Armah's* case was about an order made by a metropolitan magistrate. Lord Reid's observations therein on jurisdiction have been thought to be of limited scope: *R. v. Bedwellty Justices, ex p. Williams* [1996] 3 W.L.R. 361, 369; [1996] 3 All E.R. 737, 744–5.

may not matter greatly, as Lord Diplock's exposition is in the ascendant. Diplock recognised that with a court of law there is not the same reason for leaning towards the view that Parliament would not have meant to confer a power to decide [sc. conclusively] questions of law. This part of his speech in *Racal* has an uncharacteristic ambiguity, but it may be understood to indicate that it is only where there is a privative clause ("where the decision of the court is made final and conclusive by the statute") that the former subtle and confusing distinctions survive. On that understanding, his remarks are in harmony with the policy of Parliament embodied in the Tribunals and Inquiries Act 1992, section 12(2)(a). Further and importantly, that is the understanding of Lord Browne-Wilkinson in *ex p. Page*.[30]

I must freely acknowledge that by this stage of the present discussion any more-or-less ordinary representatives of the Common People of England would have abandoned any attempt at comprehension. Miss Hamlyn's wishes would be frustrated in that respect. Whether any Fellow of All Souls has or would have remained in better touch can only be a matter for speculation. Yet in the end a simple proposition does emerge. It is that a reviewing court can always correct what it regards as errors of law by an administrative tribunal or authority, or by an inferior court expected to apply the general law of the land, provided only in the case of the latter that there is no privative clause. If there is a privative clause, the power to review the inferior court's decision is still limited in ways which it remains as difficult as ever to define. I believe that on the whole the Common People would expect some such position as this. It would be generally understood that the higher courts are there partly to settle the law in doubtful cases.[31]

AN AUSTRALIAN DEVIATION

Sadly I have to mention that the waters have become rather muddied again in Australia. In *Craig v. State of South Australia*[32] the High Court were concerned with a fairly simple situation. A District Court Judge had stayed the hearing of criminal informations on the ground that the prisoner, through no fault on his

[30] [1993] A.C. at 703.
[31] As was in effect recognised by the subsequent legislative history of a Government proposal to override *Anisminic*; see Blom-Cooper and Drewry *Final Appeal* (Clarendon Press, Oxford, 1972) 265.
[32] (1995) 131 A.L.R. 595.

own part, had been unable so far to obtain legal representation. Controversy about the scope of the legal aid scheme seems to have been in the background. The Supreme Court of the State, by a majority decision, quashed the stay by *certiorari*. On appeal to the High Court that result was reversed and the stay restored. From the account of the facts contained in the unanimous judgment of the High Court it would seem to have been a straightforward instance of a finding by a District Court Judge not shown to have misapprehended the law in any way and supported by evidence. But, instead of disposing of the case on that basis, the High Court chose to undertake a general survey of the law of jurisdiction, almost but not quite reinventing the wheel. Not quite, because they treated Lord Reid's speech in *Anisminic* as confined to administrative tribunals and not extending to inferior courts of law. And, of more concern, as to inferior courts of law they did not merely say that in Australia the esoteric distinctions survive (the High Court's own words were that in some cases the line between jurisdictional error and mere error "may be particularly difficult to discern"). They also made no reference at all to privative clauses, thus apparently leaving the Australian law regarding inferior curial jurisdiction with all the old difficulties, even when there is no privative clause. Moreover they adopted an exceedingly narrow concept of the record, holding that references in a court's formal order such as "for the reasons given" do not incorporate the reasons.

The whole subject bristles with difficulties, of course, and any suggestion by me about the law of Australia must be gratuitous and intrusive. I am nevertheless fortified by being able to add that the former Chief Justice of Australia, Sir Anthony Mason, joined with me in a recent decision of the Supreme Court of Fiji[33] in which we were able to support our conclusion by either *ex p. Page* or *Craig v. South Australia*. An election was unnecessary, but some readers of our judgment may discern a preference for *Page*. It is as well that the High Court of Australia judgment is delivered in a form veiling the identity of the member of the Court who was the principal author. All that can be said is that it was a joint enterprise of five; and their names can be suppressed here, which is desirable as your lecturer hopes to retain all his very good friends in Canberra. It may do no harm, although it may also do little good, to add that the difficulties can often be resolved by the discretion

[33] *Ponsami v. Reddy* (September 1996)

77

invariably associated with modern judicial review. A reviewing court can hold its hand if there is or was provision for appeal. If not (which was *Craig*'s case) a privative clause may be allowed to protect the inferior court's decision except for more blatant forms of error. If neither privative clause nor right of appeal, judicial review for material error of law should be available.

CONSTITUTIONAL BEDROCK

We have seen that, in England, the rule of administrative law is now settled that questions of law are always ultimately for the courts. The refinement that an error of law by an inferior court, at least if not sufficiently apparent, may be shielded by a privative clause does not derogate from the rule. To join good company in stating the blindingly obvious (see the third lecture), an inferior court is a court. The reason why the rule is of profound importance is that is a manifestation of a fundamental constitutional principle—perhaps the only truly fundamental principle of the British constitution. Often that description is reserved for the sovereignty of Parliament.[34] But, almost as often as the question is carefully examined, it is demonstrated that the sovereignty of Parliament is a doctrine evolved *by the courts*, based on their judgment of political reality. That so-called ultimate legal principle or grundnorm is, in the United Kingdom, a creation of the Judges. And it is for the Judges to modify it if they deem this essential, as Sir William Wade has just underlined in his article *Sovereignty—Revolution or Evolution?*[35] dealing with European Community membership.

In *Pickin v. British Railways Board*[36] Lord Reid said "The function of the court is to construe and apply the enactments of Parliament." I am not here concerned to debate his more debatable and probably unprovable suggestion[37] in the same speech that the courts would never disregard an Act of Parliament insofar as it was contrary to the law of nature. Subject to that debate, the proposition quoted might seem trite. But, seen from an aspect different from that

[34] Most recently last evening, when it found a place in Lord Steyn's lecture to the Administrative Law Bar Association advocating radical changes in the constitutional roles of the Lord Chancellor, the Home Secretary, and the Attorney-General.
[35] (1996) 112 L.Q.R. 568.
[36] [1974] A.C. 765, 787.
[37] *Ibid.* 782.

with which Lord Reid was concerned, the proposition contains a fundamental truth that may be less obvious. Adjudication on law is ultimately for the courts. Certainly the courts can be re-organised or reformed, as when the judicial functions of the House of Lords were reconstituted in the manner sketched in my first lecture, or when the Supreme Court of Judicature was created out of a number of separate courts. Changes may be made in detail. But the total abolition of an independent judiciary is unthinkable; its existence is the basic rock of the constitution. An Act wholly replacing the independent judiciary by a congeries of administrative tribunals with members holding office at the pleasure of the government of the day can scarcely be imagined; and I believe that the courts would not uphold it.[38]

Of course this does not imply that the courts have anything like autocratic or arbitrary authority. It is of the essence of their role that they defer to the political institutions in matters of broad policy, confining themselves to what are commonly called justiciable issues. No less clearly, their role must have creative elements. It always has had and always will. The exercise has to be accompanied by restraint and is a matter for judgment. In each of the first three lectures salient instances of such activity, amounting to Turning Points of the Common Law, have been considered. Among the factors to which weight has to be given can be any consequences for the public purse, as well illustrated by both the majority and the minority speeches in *Stovin v. Wise*,[39] discussed in the third lecture.

The Judges have to be and are acutely sensitive to the fact that they operate in a democracy: "a state of society characterised by recognition of equality of rights and privileges" to take one of the dictionary definitions.[40] They are non-elected, but that is part of the very point of their office. To preserve democracy, to ensure that the equality of rights and privileges is maintained as far as reasonably practicable, it is necessary to have independent Judges.

---

[38] If willing to uphold it, the Judges would be acquiescing in a revolution. If unwilling but clearly faced with a situation in which a powerful government would ignore their ruling their alternative would be resignation. Some such situations arose in *Belarus* in December 1996 and juridical resignations did occur; but the seizure of power by the President may have been to some extent sanctioned by a power referendum.

[39] [1996] A.C. at 923; [1996] 3 W.L.R. 388; [1996] 3 All E.R. 801.

[40] From Chambers Dictionary.

That is the context in which and the postulate on which the Common People of the United Kingdom vote.

Fourth Hamlyn Lecture
November 28, 1996
All Souls College, Oxford

Appendix – *The Times* Crossword

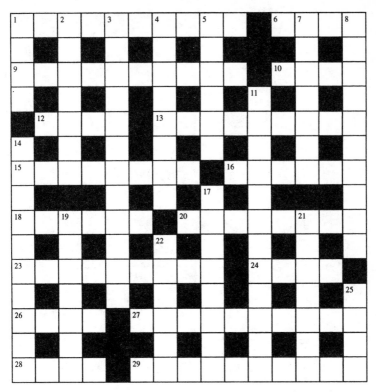

ACROSS

1 Favour ending with clue that's different (10)
6 Inspect second prison (4)
9 Repentance of offender in tort
I mishandled (10)
10 On TV, spots English novelist (4)
12 Item included by typical solicitor (4)
13 Jude involved in charge of intolerance (9)
15 A hard case is a bad one for houseman? (8)
16 Lodge is home - last resort (6)
18 A mouthpiece in church for religious ruler (6)
20 Scot endlessly making noise
about partners (8)
23 Skilled workers applied mathematics (9)
24 Settles first parts of policy, as you see (4)
26 Don Juan making love in the French way? (4)
27 Notice old German holding back drug,
so act as judge (10)
28 Murder victim, unmarried woman (4)
29 Totally confused as you try TV broadcast
without extra information (5-5)

DOWN

1 Island appearing to make slow progress (4)
2 Parts of England once, and most
of Wales? Wrong (7)
3 Sort of old apparel for a judge (4,2,6)
4 Legal principle about street people revised (8)
5 Vessel used by explorer with hesitation (6)
7 One sent down-under, once (7)
8 Fresh enthusiasm also found in
these islands (3,7)
11 Bend the head for a crucial moment (7,5)
14 Jet woman provided as transport
for prisoners (5,5)
17 Nobody's, do we hear, in this college? (3,5)
19 Talk from the French priest about
theology, initially (7)
21 Just under a month to provide this piece
of capital (7)
22 Asian using old-fashioned spell in celebration
inside house (6)
25 Light and jolly (4)

© THE TIMES 1996

Appendix – *The Times* Crossword

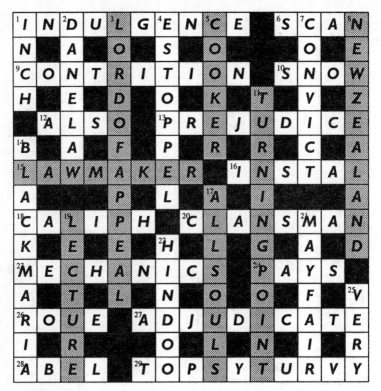

ACROSS

1 Favour ending with clue that's different (10)
6 Inspect second prison (4)
9 Repentance of offender in tort I mishandled (10)
10 On TV, spots English novelist (4)
12 Item included by typical solicitor (4)
13 Jude involved in charge of intolerance (9)
15 A hard case is a bad one for houseman? (8)
16 Lodge is home - last resort (6)
18 A mouthpiece in church for religious ruler (6)
20 Scot endlessly making noise about partners (8)
23 Skilled workers applied mathematics (9)
24 Settles first parts of policy, as you see (4)
26 Don Juan making love in the French way? (4)
27 Notice old German holding back drug, so act as judge (10)
28 Murder victim, unmarried woman (4)
29 Totally confused as you try TV broadcast without extra information (5-5)

DOWN

1 Island appearing to make slow progress (4)
2 Parts of England once, and most of Wales? Wrong (7)
3 Sort of old apparel for a judge (4,2,6)
4 Legal principle about street people revised (8)
5 Vessel used by explorer with hesitation (6)
7 One sent down-under, once (7)
8 Fresh enthusiasm also found in these islands (3,7)
11 Bend the head for a crucial moment (7,5)
14 Jet woman provided as transport for prisoners (5,5)
17 Nobody's, do we hear, in this college? (3,5)
19 Talk from the French priest about theology, initially (7)
21 Just under a month to provide this piece of capital (7)
22 Asian using old-fashioned spell in celebration inside house (6)
25 Light and jolly (4)

INDEX

Index

Learning Resources
Centre